# *Advance Praise*

"Stephen Smith is a highly engaging, sympathetic and humorous everyman, addressing adventures and situations most folks have had, such as being an All American college-boy-or-girl-home-on-break worker in retail over the Christmas holidays. His experiences as a Drug Fair Veg-O-Matic salesman come to us with hilarious dry-wit and droll delivery. So memorable – and heartwarming to the maximum!"

—Bland Simpson, author of *North Carolina: Land of Water, Land of Sky*

"Stephen Smith's new memoir is loaded with whip-smart humor, keen insights into a college kid trying to figure things out, and reminiscences of a time and place that leave you smiling and musing, 'Yes, that's the way it was.' This book is a great read. Jaunty, delightful, wonderfully absorbing, impossible to resist. The writing simply shines."

—Judy Goldman, author of *Child: A Memoir*

"One of the enduring pleasures of my life is that I get to read Stephen E. Smith on a regular basis. We should all be so lucky. His poetry is sublime and his prose is witty, charming, poignant and crafted with the consummate skill of a P.G. Wodehouse, one of the writers he cherished as a young man. *The Year We Danced: A Memoir* is sweet and funny and profoundly us. If you love a tale, or tales, well told, this is the book for you."

—Jim Moriarty, editor, *PineStraw* magazine

"Would you buy a Vega-O-Magic from this man? If 'this man' is Stephen Smith, the answer is emphatically YES! Smith's humorous tone and talent for the absurd make him and this book companionable and delightful. Smith is a reliably hilarious storyteller."

—Paul Jones, author of *Something Wonderful*

# The Year We Danced

# The Year We Danced

*a memoir*

Stephen E. Smith

Copyright © 2024 by Stephen E. Smith

All rights reserved. No part of this book may be reproduced or transmitted in any form or by any means, electronic or mechanical, including photocopy, recording, or any information storage and retrieval system, without prior permission from the publisher (except by reviewers who may quote brief passages).

First Edition

Hardcover ISBN: 978-1-62720-537-5
Paperback ISBN: 978-1-62720-538-2
Ebook ISBN: 978-1-62720-539-9

Design by Apprentice House
Editorial Development by Matthew Gamerdinger
Promotional Development by Eisa Abu-Sbaih

Published by Apprentice House Press

Loyola University Maryland
4501 N. Charles Street, Baltimore, MD 21210
410.617.5265
www.ApprenticeHouse.com

info@ApprenticeHouse.com

Some of these chapters appeared in the following periodicals: *North Carolina Literary Review, Salt, O.Henry, PineStraw,* and *The Pilot.*

*For Steve Tindall, Gene Matthews, Scott Roberson, Witt Halle, Steve Maynard, Jim Brinkley, and the other palookas on the second floor of Smith dorm, wherever they are.*

. . . we uttered the names that had been silent upon our lips for fifty years, and it was as if they were made of music; with reverent hands we unburied our dead, the mates of our youth, and caressed them with our speech; we searched the dusty chambers of our memories and dragged forth incident after incident, episode after episode, folly after folly, and laughed such good laughs over them, with the tears running down . . . .

—*Autobiography of Mark Twain*

# Author's Note

When SARS-CoV-2 descended upon us in March 2020, the world as I'd known it shut down. I ordered groceries on my computer, avoided the doctor's office, ceased to meet with friends, gave greenway joggers a wide berth. I'd been working from home for years, writing book reviews and magazine features, but I was suddenly locked in place, awaiting the disappearance of the virus or the arrival of an effective vaccine. Thus isolated, I began to ponder a new writing project, one that would allow me to forget (at least momentarily) the increasing rate of infection and skyrocketing death statistics. The answer was obvious: why not write a brief memoir about the most interesting time of my life, my freshman year in college? Surely that would cheer me up. For 30 years, I'd been writing occasional humorous magazine and newspaper features about that very subject.

When I decided to pull the material together into something resembling a narrative, I consulted primary sources: the notebooks I kept from September 1965 to June 1966, the months during which I was a freshman at little Elon College in North Carolina. At that moment in my young life it was never my intention to keep a journal, but as I'd jotted down the salient points of class lectures,

I'd also tracked my expenditures, inserted pertinent notes and newspaper and magazine clippings, doodled caricatures of faculty and students, and scribbled brief comments concerning my social life, e.g., "Hitchhike to Tap Room with Tindall and Gene this afternoon," or "Date Sat. to Castaways." Although I never detailed what occurred during these outings, these brief notations triggered synaptic connections that might have otherwise eluded me.

While the characters in this memoir are living and breathing beings, I have, in a few instances, employed pseudonyms and altered descriptions to avoid embarrassing old friends and acquaintances. In transcribing dialogue, I've relied on my ability to recall conversations with a reasonable degree of accuracy. When unsure about phraseology, I attempted to recreate the words we spoke by recalling the context of our conversations.

Nothing conjures up a scene or an image like a keepsake. A defunct harmonica (key of C), a pay stub from Drug Fair, two unopened packs of Home Run cigarettes, two letters from my father, copies of manipulative notes I'd written to my parents requesting money, and six books, including a *Harbrace College Handbook* and a paperback of P.G. Wodehouse's *The Brinkmanship of Galahad Threepwood*, have survived in a battered cardboard box stored in the attics of the homes I'd occupied over the years. A Harris Tweed sports jacket, required attire for Saturday dinners on campus, has hung in my closet for more than half a century. Tucked in the breast pocket is a folded napkin listing the songs I danced to during my first visit to Greensboro's Castaways club in February 1966. Together they offer a vague transcription of my life during those distant days and nights.

Memoir, like all autobiography, is a form of confession and as such tends to be self-serving, but I've held back little, good or bad, honorable and otherwise, of what befell me during that time.

Probably there were things I did and shouldn't have done, things I've forgotten, and things I should have done but didn't. The trifling difficulties I encountered during those playful and sometimes painful days of 1965–66, events that once struck me as significant, have become a source of consolation when considering the trials we all confront in this new world. I hope old college friends—indeed, anyone who has fully embraced the chance of life—will find in these pages a remembrance of the brief, sudden, beautiful awakenings we experienced.

# The Year We Danced Soundtrack

"96 Tears" by ? and the Mysterians
"All My Loving" by The Beatles
"A Lover's Concerto" by The Toys
"Ballad of the Green Berets" by Barry Sadler
"Catch the Wind" by Donovan
"Double Shot (of My Baby's Love)" by The Swinging Medallions
"Down in the Boondocks" by Billy Joe Royal
"Do You Believe in Magic" by The Lovin' Spoonful
"Eve of Destruction" by Barry McGuire
"For Your Love" by Yardbirds
"Goin' Out of My Head" by Little Anthony and the Imperials
"Good Lovin'" by The Young Rascals
"Goodnight, Irene" by The Weavers
"Hang on Sloopy" by The McCoys
"Hanky Panky" by Tommy James and Shondells
"Heart of Stone" by The Rolling Stones
"Heat Wave" by Martha and the Vandellas
"Hey! Baby" by Bruce Channel
"Hey! I Know You" by Monzas
"Hot Cha" by Junior Walker & the All Stars
"Hurt So Bad" by Little Anthony and the Imperials

"(I Can't Get No) Satisfaction" by The Rolling Stones
"If I Didn't Have a Dime" by Bob Collins and the Fabulous Five
"I'll Be Doggone" by Marvin Gaye
"I Love Onions" by Susan Christie
"I'm a King Bee" by The Rolling Stones
"I Saw Her Again" by The Mamas and the Papas
"It's All Right" by The Impressions
"Let the Good Times Roll" by Shirley and Lee
"Li'l Red Riding Hood" by Sam the Sham and the Pharaohs
"London Bridge Is Falling Down" trad.
"Mustang Sally" by Wilson Pickett
"My Girl" by Temptations
"Paint It Black" by The Rolling Stones
"Rag Doll" by Frankie Valli and the Four Seasons
"Ring Around the Rosie" trad.
"Shady Grove" trad.
"Shotgun" by Junior Walker and the All Stars
"Sixty Minute Man" by Billie Ward and the Dominos
"Stop! In the Name of Love" by The Supremes
"Stubborn Kind of Fellow" by Marvin Gaye
"Summer in the City" by The Lovin' Spoonful
"Tears on My Pillow" by Little Anthony and the Imperials
"Thank You John" by Willie Tee
"The More I See You" by Chris Montez
"The Tennessee Waltz" by Redd Stewart and Pee Wee King
"Time Won't Let Me" by The Outsiders
"Tracks of My Tears" by Smokey Robinson and the Miracles
"Unchained Melody" by The Righteous Bros
"Under the Boardwalk" by The Drifters
"We Can Work It Out" by The Beatles
"(What a Day for a) Daydream" by The Lovin' Spoonful

"What Goes On" by The Beatles
"Wild Thing" by the Troggs
"Wildwood Flower" by The Carter Family

August 1965-January 1966

# One

By late August, I had it figured out: The state of North Carolina is located south of Virginia and north of South Carolina. I was sure of that. I'd also acquired a tenuous grasp of Southern culture by reading the lascivious passages in *God's Little Acre* and by watching *Gone with the Wind* at the Playhouse Theater in my hometown of Annapolis, Maryland. Southerners were either dangerously inbred or they were in the habit of devouring raw turnips and swearing, "As God is my witness . . ." or whatever it is Scarlett snarls into the lens as the sun sets forever on the Confederacy. I'd seen the Birmingham police dogs and fire hoses on TV news, and on Saturday nights the AM radio crackled and hummed with brimstone-spewing Elmer Gantrys. But the South I imagined—the South I *needed* to believe in—was all magnolia-scented twilights populated with petulant belles who finger-curled their golden tresses and sighed, "Oh my, how you Yankee cads do set our poor Southern hearts aflutter." When I was 18, clichés were the stuff of truth.

I'd graduated from high school in June of '65, and that summer I was working forty-eight hours a week as a cashier at a Safeway store, saving every cent to pay my college tuition. My father had taken charge of my college application process the previous March, and he announced at the dinner table on the first Wednesday in June that I'd be headed south in the fall. We were devouring Mrs. Paul's fish sticks and oven-baked frozen French fries smothered in Hunt's ketchup, our standard Wednesday evening fare, when he stared at me across the dinner table and stated matter-of-factly, "You're going to North Carolina in the fall."

I froze in mid-bite, a flaky chunk of trans-fat-engorged fish stick balanced on my fork. "I am?"

"Yeah, you're going to Elon College," he continued. "It's far enough away that you won't be running home every fifteen minutes."

"Tell me the name of the college again?" I asked.

My friends had normal fathers who had regular jobs such as insurance agent or shoe salesman, but my father was the boxing coach at the United States Naval Academy. In his world, midshipmen snapped to attention and barked "Aye, aye, sir." He wasn't crazy mean like the badass Marine drill sergeants I had seen in the movies, and I hadn't grown up with mental or physical abuse, but he brooked no back sass, especially at the dinner table. Even asking an inoffensive question could be risky, depending on his mood.

He didn't bother to answer my question but glared at me, a frown wrinkling his broad forehead and a tautness swelling his jowls, an expression I associated with impending emotional discomfort. He was anticipating protestations to his startling announcement, and his stern countenance was meant to discourage any objections I might have. His oversized ears stuck straight out from his buzz-cut skull and his crooked nose, broken in a boxing match when he was thirteen, hung hook-like between his eyes. He was not to be trifled with.

"Elon College," my mother said. Her facial expression, calm but cautious, was less alarming, indicating that the information I'd been handed might not be life-threatening. She had bright auburn hair and a fiery temperament to match, and she usually interceded on my behalf when my father's disposition was taking a perilous turn. If this news was detrimental to my well-being, she would have said so. Instead, she pursed her lips, silently urging me to keep my mouth shut.

"Where's this college he's going to?" my sixteen-year-old sister, Debbie, interjected, crunching on a French fry. Mike, my eleven-year-old freckle-faced, redheaded brother, who'd been diagnosed by our mother as hyperactive in utero, sensed a probable domestic disturbance and prudently abandoned the table.

"Can't you excuse yourself?" my mother called after him, but Mike was out the back door before her words overtook him. It was wise to make tracks when the old man was about to go on a tear, and we were, perhaps, at a tipping point.

"I thought he was going to go to the community college like everybody else," my sister said.

I'd succeeded in remaining almost invisible at home during my senior year in high school, due largely to my sister's wild-child behavior. Her curly brown hair, easy smile, and audacious temperament ensured her popularity among her peers, especially her male friends, but her proclivity for attaching herself to rowdy suitors made her the sole recipient of our household's tenuous parenting skills.

"You stay out of this," our father snapped.

I didn't have the slightest objection to my father's news; I merely wanted to know the name of the college. I was thankful I'd soon be a freshman instead of a buck private, an option that he touted as an appealing alternative to higher education. My friend Barrie Barnes had shipped off to basic training immediately after high school graduation and my father frequently reminded me that Barrie was "having the time of his life in the army."

*The time of his life.* I wasn't buying that fairy tale.

The Barnes family were longtime friends who lived in Salisbury, Maryland, and Barrie, a few weeks younger than I, was a big lug of a kid, at least 6'4" and weighing in at 230 pounds. We'd grown up together in the little Delmarva town of Easton before our families relocated, and now he was sweating out basic training somewhere in the Deep South. At my mother's insistence, I'd written Barrie a brief note asking how he was enjoying army life, and he'd sent me a plain white postcard with this emphatic message: "Its [sic] hell!!!!" which contradicted my father's brief, enticing depiction of the army experience. I was taking Barrie's word for it.

"It's called Elon," my father said. "Look it up."

A couple of weeks after my father announced where I'd be continuing my education, I was slouched behind my cash register at the Safeway calculating the price for two cans of pickled beets that sold for 7/$2.26 when I was overcome with a desire to obtain more information about the college where I'd presumably be spending the next four years. The cans of beets, like my future, were bearing down on me with alarming alacrity, and I thought: seven goes into twenty-two three times, which is twenty-one, carry the one—and whoosh! I shoved the cans by my register faster than Einstein could calculate the price per unit—and I didn't charge the customer a red cent. I no longer cared about being a trusted Safeway employee, or for that matter, a good son, brother or friend or anything else that had to do with the life I'd be leaving behind. My time in Annapolis was nearing an end, and I had to get a handle on this college business.

Five minutes later, I approached Mr. Short, the Safeway's skeletal, laconic manager, feigning illness. "I've got a terrible sore throat that's probably contagious; I don't want anyone else to catch it," I croaked—and then hoofed it to the city library on Church Circle, where I plundered through the reference section until I happened upon an out-of-date paperback aptly titled *The College Sourcebook*. I leafed through the well-worn pages to a brief entry on Elon College: "... a church-related, liberal arts institution located in the Piedmont," wherever and whatever that was. Inserted in the text was a blurry black-and-white photograph that captured a post-World War II couple lolling away an afternoon in the shadow of a huge bent oak. The casually attired fair-haired boy had propped his oxford-clad left foot on a concrete bench where a smiling "coed," shapeless in crinolines and a fluffy sweater, stared wistfully into his eyes as he focused on the bright and shining future unfolding before him. Since I was most concerned about my social life at college—I had no idea what I'd be studying and didn't care—I found the photograph mildly encouraging. It was apparent that male-female relationships were an accepted part of campus life. That was good news.

I grabbed a tattered 1940s Rand McNally atlas from the stacks, found Elon in the index, and traced its location on the map. North Carolina was bigger than I'd expected, more than four times the size of Maryland, taking up two pages of the atlas. Elon was a tiny dot in the north-central section of the state, a speck that took a minute or two to locate. To the east of the college lay Burlington, a town, according to the map's color code, smaller than Annapolis, but to the west the City of Greensboro was a yellow blob with a population of at least 100,000.

I immediately looked up Greensboro in an encyclopedia and read a brief explanation of the thriving textile and tobacco industries, and then ran my finger down a list of colleges located in the city. When I got to an entry for Woman's College of North Carolina, I encountered this astonishing sentence: "Woman's

College is the largest all-female university in the United States." When I read those words, I closed the encyclopedia and sat straight up in my chair and snorted. I was no high-octane lady killer in high school, but I'd had my fair share of girlfriends and had grown to appreciate the company of freethinking women. I saw no reason to deprive myself of a good time while in college. I expected to do my share of studying to maintain my 2-S draft classification, but there would be weekends when I could do as I pleased. I was looking forward to making a complete fool of myself in front of as many Southern belles as humanly possible.

I'd learned from acquaintances who'd completed their first year of college that freshman males were *persona non grata* on campus, so I knew I'd stand little chance with the girls at Elon. I was a primate living in a hierarchical society, and as a college freshman, I knew I'd be low man on the linear distribution, but with *the largest all-female university in the United States* a stone's throw away from the college I'd be attending, the odds of my attracting a desirable woman were much improved. It was simple supply and demand, the selfsame principle that forced Safeway to sell pickled beets for 7/$2.26. Using the tip of my pinky, I estimated the distance between Elon and Greensboro, which didn't appear to be more than twenty-five miles, a negotiable distance for a teenage boy possessed of hormonal momentum. I returned the atlas to its place on the shelf and set about preparing myself to impress the multitude of man-hungry women incarcerated in North Carolina Woman's College.

In the mid-1960s, there were few opportunities for a kid like me to meet unattached girls. Teenagers weren't allowed in bars (the drinking age in Maryland was twenty-one) so in high school I dated classmates or strays I'd met when a bevy of adventurous, marginally desirable girls turned up at one of the local beach pavilions.

Any relationship, local or otherwise, was innocent in fact if not in intent, so dancing was the mechanism whereby I might impress a female. I wasn't schooled in ballroom or tap dancing or even the basic box step, but I knew how to get down and dirty with a few inappropriate moves—provocative gyrations that were, I thought at that moment in my life, the soul of roguishness.

I visualize the evolution of dance in the '50s and '60s in the manner biology textbooks illustrated the evolution of man, beginning with the emergent Gibbon-like humanoid evolving into the upright Homo sapiens. From our earliest years, baby boomers were raised as dancers, starting with "Ring Around the Rosie" and "London Bridge Is Falling Down" and progressing to the Hokey Pokey, the Bunny Hop, the Twist, the Cha-Cha, the Stroll, The Madison, the Hully Gully, the Pony, the Dirty Dog, and other long-forgotten contortions that are now laughable when viewed on ancient Kinescope clips.

Music was the highway on which pop culture traveled, and for those of us who came of age in the Baltimore-Washington-Annapolis triangle, that road led to *The Buddy Deane Show*, an *American Bandstand* knockoff that aired weekday afternoons on WJZ-TV (the program was the model on which John Waters based *Hairspray*). I picked up the various dances by watching teenagers lay down their best steps on black-and-white TV, and when I attended high school dances, I imitated my Baltimore betters. By the end of my junior year, *The Buddy Deane Show* was canceled when Buddy refused to integrate the program (the opposite of what happens in *Hairspray*), and the Beatles had deplaned and appeared on *The Ed Sullivan Show*. That was the end of dance crazes. The fab four made it acceptable for teenagers to gyrate however they pleased. Life went free-form.

If the Beatles persuaded us to grow our hair long, the Rolling

Stones encouraged anything outrageous. "I'm a King Bee" was way surlier than "All My Loving," and by the summer of '64 the dancers in Annapolis were whirling dervishes performing an interpretive variation of the Freddie. But dancing is a fickly business, and by the summer of '65, the signature Annapolis step had gone minimalist in repetition and iteration, stripped to its essential elements, which meant it was cool to hardly move a muscle on the dance floor. I'd stand with my feet shoulder-width apart, my knees slightly bent, and my lilted hands held at waist level where they would shift back and forth imperceptibly as if I were conjuring up Beelzebub. I had every reason to believe that teenage girls in North Carolina—and most particularly the wanton females at Woman's College—would appreciate the subtle moves I was putting down. It was a question of getting it just right.

So after my trip to the library, I began knocking off work early on Friday nights. I'd change into shorts and a T-shirt in the Safeway stockroom and drive my cantankerous '53 Chrysler Windsor five miles to Sparrow's Beach, where I'd dance the night away to the astringent strains of Norman's Norts. On twilight August evenings, a warm breeze wafted off the Chesapeake as I pulled into the dusty pavilion parking lot to the primal three-note guitar riff of the Stones' "(I Can't Get No) Satisfaction" or the jangle of the Yardbirds' "For Your Love." Adventurous females from chic Severna Park or the wilds of Glen Burnie drifted around the dance floor in bustling constellations, and I'd select an attractive stranger and ask her if she'd like to dance. If she did, I put down my best Annapolis steps, demonstrating my subtle, visceral response to the music.

Hanging out at Sparrow's Beach also allowed me to hone my communication skills. After I'd danced with a girl once or twice, there was usually an opportunity to exchange pleasantries. I have no idea what we talked about—it couldn't have been very cerebral; we knew next to nothing—but I remember the excessive use of the intensifiers such as "you know," "like," "far out" and "groovy." If the girl was from out of town, we'd mention someone who knew someone who maybe knew someone until the Norts blasted the humid night air with a churlish rendition of "Heart of Stone," and we'd take to the dance floor again.

With my steps down solid and my conversational skills perfected, I spent the last week in August selecting the clothing required to make myself irresistible. I possessed much of the gear—"the uniform," my mother called it—three pairs of khaki slacks; two pairs of Levi's cords; a brown belt; button-down shirts in blue, white, yellow, and faded madras; and Weejun loafers, which I wore sockless. All I needed was a new sports jacket. My father offered to take me to Robert Hall, first of the big-box men's clothing stores, to purchase a $49.95 suit, but I refused, opting instead for a trip to a clothier on Maryland Avenue to select a Harris Tweed sports jacket that was more to my liking. I had to pay for it myself, but it was worth the expenditure to know I had what was required for an active social life.

As the date for my departure for college drew near, I was confident that all was well with the world—until I stepped through the front door at 6:20 p.m. on the first Monday in September to find my mother and father waiting for me in the living room. As I made my entrance, they dropped whatever they'd been discussing, an indication I might be in serious trouble.

My father was stretched out on the couch in a pair of white boxer shorts and a white T-shirt with NAVY embossed across the breast, his standard attire while lounging about the house in the summer. My mother sat in an antique rocker, her countenance one of mild concern.

"Is something wrong?" I asked.

"Your grandmother is coming to see you tomorrow," my father said, his tone accusatory. "She wants to talk with you before you go to college."

"Grandmother Drager?" I asked. It would hardly be news if my maternal grandmother was coming for a visit. She and my grandfather McKnett lived in Easton, an hour away, and she was in and out of our house often. But my Grandmother Drager (she married Larry Drager after divorcing my Grandfather Smith in the late '40s) lived in Kent, Ohio, and in my eighteen years, she'd visited with us on only three or four occasions.

"Yes, your Grandmother Drager," my father said, suggesting I was somehow responsible for her visit. "What do you suppose she wants?"

I shrugged. "Gosh, how would I know? I can't remember the last time I talked to her."

"Well, she'll be here tomorrow afternoon on the bus," he said, sitting up on the couch.

"What in the world," my mother asked, "are we going to do with her for three days?"

My mother enjoyed a visceral contempt for every member of my father's family. She referred to them collectively as "the nutheads," and with good reason. My Grandfather Smith, the nominal head of the clan, was a recovering alcoholic, and according to family lore, he'd enjoyed numerous affairs while he was married to my grandmother. During Prohibition he'd disappear for days to pursue the sporting life—gambling, drinking, carousing—and when he returned home, he'd force his children to give up their beds to the bums he'd befriended while on his bender. Cousins, uncles, aunts, and the other nutheads, had pursued strange religious practices and dabbled in all manner of hocus-pocus. One was a pet hoarder. My father's great uncle, a deaf mute, had beaten a mule to death with a two-by-four and spent the remainder of his life in an asylum—and he was a saner member of the Smith bunch. My father's Uncle Wilbur had run away from home in the early '30s to join a religious cult. He'd ridden the rails back to Kent in 1935 only to find that life in Ohio remained desperate. When he tried to escape the family turmoil by jumping a freight, he fell between the cars and was decapitated.

A particularly memorable anecdote featuring my Ohio grandmother as an amateur sleuth was my mother's favorite nuthead tale. My grandfather had been keeping company with a preacher's wife, and when my grandmother got word of an impending tryst at the local presbytery, she latched on to the spare tire on the back of my grandfather's Model A and was transported down Water Street, the main thoroughfare of Kent, as my grandfather motored to his romantic rendezvous. Anxious to bed his lover, Grandfather Smith parked his car in the preacher's driveway and disappeared into the parsonage. When my grandmother was sure the lovers had taken to the preacher's bed, she burst into the house discharging a pistol she'd secreted on her person, forcing the fornicating couple to flee naked out the back door. How the encounter ended, I was never told, but my mother offered the anecdote as an example of the lack of moral rectitude prevalent among the Ohio Smiths.

Marital hijinks aside, I had a deep affection for my paternal grandmother. She was loving and unfailingly generous. When I was five, she gifted me a 12-volume set of beautifully illustrated *My Bookhouse Books*, which I read for the next ten years. The books included wonderful stories, poems, and biographies arranged from nursery to junior high school and much of the English-language canon was included. She transformed me into a lifelong reader. There could have been no greater gift.

When my grandparents divorced, my grandmother married Larry Drager, a gentleman so afflicted with Parkinson's that it took him forty-five excruciating minutes to shuffle the ten feet from his easy chair to the dinner table. To overawe the slightest hint of iniquity in her new life, my grandmother scrubbed and cleaned and shined and hid unused cakes of aromatic Sweetheart soap in strategic locations around her home. She never forgave her wayward first husband and never passed up a chance to deliver a sermon on the evils of drink. When she referred to my grandfather, which was often and always in the most derogatory terms, she'd conclude her remarks with, "I tell you what's the truth: A good man gone wrong is a bad man found out."

"I can't imagine what she would have to say to Stephen," my mother said.

My father shook his head. "It must be important for her to ride three-hundred-fifty miles on the bus with a bunch of trashy people. Something's up. She didn't have much in the way of advice when I went off to college. She handed me an old dictionary and said, 'Hit the road.'"

The following evening, I drove our Ford Fairlane to the bus station on West Street. My parents had insisted that I pick up Grandma Drager so she could deliver her homily as the two of us rode back to the house. The sooner they discovered the object of her visit the better.

I was sitting in the car listening to WCAO on the radio when the Greyhound rumbled into the parking lot, tilted dangerously to one side, and expelled a noxious burst of diesel exhaust. The air brakes hissed and the bus wobbled to a stop. The door folded inward and Grandmother Drager popped out like a cuckoo, followed by an eclectic jumble of bedraggled travelers.

My grandmother was of medium height and a trifle

overweight. She wore gold-colored wire-rimmed glasses on her round face, which was usually graced with a quizzical smile that suggested she was privy to a secret she might divulge if you told her what she wanted to hear, which was, of course, that my grandfather was a jerk. Her curly bobbed hair was shiny and silvery-white and over-processed. She was decked out in her Sunday best, a dark blue flower-patterned buttoned-up dress and a clunky pair of black leather lace-up shoes with thick two-inch heels. An enormous black purse dangled from her arm. She stepped onto the asphalt and paused, searching for a familiar face. As I approached, she smiled broadly and said, "Let your old grandma give you a kiss on your fat cheek," and she grabbed my skull with both hands and smooched my jowl.

I retrieved her luggage from the bus driver, catching a whiff of Sweetheart soap as he handed me her cardboard suitcases, and opened the Fairlane's passenger-side door for her. As we rounded Church Circle and coasted down Duke of Gloucester Street, she held forth on the deficiencies of her fellow travelers.

"Apparently, they don't sell deodorant where these people come from," she said. "Nobody is considerate anymore. The woman in the seat next to me stank to high heaven and wouldn't shut up. Talk, talk, talk. As far as I'm concerned that's one of the problems with the world—people talking too much." She paused, then added, "And there was a sailor who was drinking whisky from a bottle in a dirty paper sack. I asked what he was drinking and he said it was soda, but I know what whisky smells like." She cut her eyes in my direction. "Your grandfather, he smelled like whisky. I'll tell you the truth: When terrible things happen to people, it's usually whisky behind every bit of it. A drunken sailor on the bus! Can you imagine? What's the world coming to?" This from a woman who rode down the main street of her hometown while hanging on to a spare tire, a blue-steel gat stuffed in her bodice.

"Gosh, I don't know," I answered.

"And *nobody* dresses up anymore when they travel. They look like a bunch of Skid Row bums. You know why people turn into Skid Row bums, don't you?"

"No, ma'am."

"It's because all they want to do is drink whisky. Your grandfather was that way."

After we pulled into the driveway, my father unloaded Grandmother Drager's perfumed suitcases and escorted her to my sister's bedroom. "Debbie can sleep on the sofa bed in the basement," he said.

My mother immediately took me aside in the kitchen. "What did she say to you?"

"She complained about the people on the bus and how Grandfather was a drunk."

Two days passed. I walked to work each morning and back home in the evenings. At dinner we ate our spaghetti and meatballs, fish sticks, or boiled hot dogs, gourmet fare at our table, but my grandmother said not one word to me. We listened to her moan and groan, discoursing on the world's imperfections and how everything was my grandfather's fault. What we wanted to hear, what we were anticipating, was the wisdom she'd come to impart.

On the final evening of her visit, Grandmother Drager carefully arranged her knife and fork on her empty dinner plate and said to me, "Stephen, let's go into the family room. I have something to say to you."

My father, mother, and sister looked up, their eyes wide with anticipation, their mouths agape. My brother, wise beyond his years, had already fled into the backyard.

"Yes, ma'am," I said, and followed her down the steps for our much-anticipated confab.

"Close the door behind you," she ordered, investing the occasion with even greater significance. She collapsed in my father's recliner, and I sat on the couch.

"Well," she said, "you'll be going off to college, and that's a big step for any young man—an important moment in your life."

"Yes, ma'am."

"You'll be meeting lots of interesting people and making new friends, and you'll have a whole new life."

"Yes, ma'am." I kept thinking: yeah, yeah, yeah, get to the point.

"Do you know that yours is the biggest generation to ever attend college? Because of the war there are a million kids who will be freshmen in college this fall. I have one piece of advice for you and all the other freshmen you meet. If you tell them this, they'll think you're a wise young man."

"Yes, ma'am."

She paused thoughtfully and leaned forward in the recliner. "Wear tennis shoes," she said.

I didn't respond immediately, suspecting that greater wisdom was to follow.

"You see," she continued after an appropriate pause, "if all the kids in college wore shoes with leather heels and soles, there would be so much noise no one could think straight. It would be awful. All that noise all day long."

"I beg your pardon," I said, suspecting I'd missed a profound sentence or two.

"You'll be contributing to all the extra noise in the world if you wear shoes with leather heels and soles. Think about it."

"Yes, ma'am." I was having difficulty processing this perplexing insight into footwear and how it applied to me and my generation.

"Promise me you'll wear tennis shoes."

"I promise," I said.

"Would you turn on the TV?" she asked, satisfied with having passed on her wisdom to one of the leaders of the twenty-first century. "Your old grandma would like to watch the news."

I switched on the TV and hurried up the stairs, closing the door behind me. My parents and sister had gathered on the landing.

"What did she say?" they asked in unison.

"She said I should wear tennis shoes when I get to college."

My parents and sister stared silently, digesting the import of Grandma's insight into the human condition. Then my parents again spoke in unison. "Tennis shoes?"

"Yeah, tennis shoes," I said.

"You mean to tell me she rode for fourteen hours on the bus from Ohio to tell you to wear tennis shoes?" my mother asked.

"I guess so."

"Nutheads," she said. "They're all nutheads."

On Thursday afternoon, I drove Grandmother Drager to the bus station so she could catch the bus to Ohio and her palsied husband. "Remember," she said, as we pulled into the parking lot, "a good man gone wrong is a bad man found out. Keep in mind what your grandma told you."

"I will," I said.

I parked the car, and she leaned across the front seat. "Let your old grandma give you a kiss on your fat cheek," she said. And she did. I watched as she climbed aboard the westbound Greyhound bus, a pudgy white-haired lady in an ill-fitting flowered dress. She turned, smiled broadly, and waved goodbye. I never saw her again.

That evening I packed for college: toiletries, clothing—yeah, a pair of tennis shoes—and all the other detritus required to survive freshman year, including my father's *Oxford English Dictionary* and *Roget's International Thesaurus of English Words and Phrases*. Into the back of my suitcase, I stuffed paperback copies of *The Mouse That Roared* by Leonard Wibberley and P.G. Wodehouse's *The Brinkmanship of Galahad Threepwood*, both of which I'd been reading in my spare time.

After clocking out at the Safeway on Friday, September 10, at 8:30 p.m., I thanked Mr. Short for giving me a job. He shook my hand and wished me well. "If you're looking for work next summer," he said, "let me know."

"I will," I replied, praying that I'd never confront another can of pickled beets.

As I walked home in the gathering dusk, friends and neighbors drove by and waved an occasional greeting. High school classes had begun the week before, and there was a home football game that evening at Weems-Whaling Field. The distant thrumming of the marching band, barely audible above the whoosh of traffic, promised autumn.

More than half a century later, I can feel that moment vividly: I'm balanced on the sheer edge of youth, poised to take that desperate leap into who-knows-what. But I'm fearless, confident I have the Southern social landscape thoroughly mapped out, nailed down, fully understood. I'm ready. And the dance floors of Carolina are wide open.

# Two

My father steered the Ford Fairlane off Haggard Avenue, through a brick-pillared, wrought iron gateway, and into the asphalt parking lot between Smith Residence Hall and the Duke Building at Elon College, North Carolina. It was 3 p.m. on the humid, overcast afternoon of Saturday, September 11, 1965. We parked near the side entrance at the north end of the dorm, a generic three-story faux-Georgian building that matched identically the Carolina Residence Hall a few hundred feet to the east.

"This is it," I said, confirming the obvious.

"Looks nice," my mother observed, craning her neck.

I'd seen photos of the building in the complimentary catalog my father had handed me that morning as we packed the station wagon. "Here," he said. "Start reading."

"How long have you had this?" I asked, knowing he'd kept the catalog from me to avoid any objections I might have voiced against his decision to banish me to North Carolina.

"I don't know, a couple of months. I forgot to give it to you."

During the seven-hour southward drive I read through the catalog, studying the black-and-white photographs of smiling students, the images of stalwart brick buildings, and reading and rereading the course descriptions, concentrating on the classes designated as required for freshmen. I memorized the campus map and the names of the buildings so that as we neared the college, I could call out directions on how to find my assigned dorm. "Turn right here and go to the end of the street. There should be a gate on the right."

Confronting the campus architecture in person, I was mildly disappointed. I hadn't expected vast stone façades and soaring buttresses (after all, Elon was a small college secreted in the somnolent South), but a few ivy-covered terra-cotta cornices would have amplified the grandeur of the buildings. Instead, these were straightforward red-brick structures connected by brick colonnades to other brick structures—forthright edifices that exuded a sensible, congenial vibe.

The parking lot was a tangle of cars disgorging parents and their addled offspring. As I stepped from the station wagon, my attention was drawn upward to the third floor of the dorm where a speaker cabinet was tilted against a window sash. Little Anthony and the Imperials' "Tears on My Pillow" cut into the humid air, and a twinge of misgiving coursed through me. If this was the music college kids in North Carolina were dancing to, my plans to impress the available female population might be in jeopardy.

My parents and I grabbed my luggage from the station wagon and struggled into the tiny first-floor lobby. The reek of sweat, dime-store perfume, and Right Guard antiperspirant permeated the muggy air. The steel and concrete staircase leading to the upper floors was awhirl with eddies of parents and freshmen hurriedly hauling boxes and suitcases in and out of the building. Music followed us upward, echoing onto the second floor, where it reverberated down the cinderblock hall.

"Sounds like a party school to me," my father said, unable to withhold his criticism any longer. "You'll never get any studying done if it's this noisy all the time." The peevish inflection in his voice indicated that he was about to pass final judgment on poor little Elon College by comparing it with the Naval Academy, and I dreaded his next sentence, which I knew would be disparaging. But what could I do? He'd signed my name to the application and submitted it to the admissions committee without my knowledge. He'd dealt this hand; now I was somehow responsible for whatever was irritating him, which was everything he'd heard and seen since pulling into the parking lot.

"They could have cleaned the place up for our arrival," he grumbled. "The floors in Bancroft Hall don't look like this, and you won't ever hear loud music playing during the day."

The dorm was a tad on the seedy side compared with the spit and polish of a military academy. Constructed of materials impervious to the violence wrought by hordes of marauding freshman boys, Smith dorm evidenced the scuffs and bruises occasioned by eight years of continuous abuse. It had rained earlier in the day, and students and their families had picked up sticky red clay on their shoes and tracked it inside so that the worn linoleum floors and rubber baseboards had acquired a dark toxic hue.

The door to 218, the room to which I'd been assigned by an anonymous secretary in the housing office, was open, and a lanky, towheaded kid was unfolding shirts and slipping them carefully onto wooden hangers. His hair was neatly combed back from his broad forehead, and his ears, like my father's, stuck out at right angles from his skull. He was dressed in the uniform of the day—khaki pants, a white button-down shirt and loafers—and he'd already staked out the left side of the room. His bed was made up with military tautness: a beige chenille bedspread stretched tight across the thin mattress and an anemic pillow fluffed against the cinderblock wall. A hardbound college dictionary and a paperback almanac were pressed between brass American eagle bookends on the outer edge of his desk, the reference works suggesting that my roommate was an earnest scholar. His dresser top was crowded with 30 or 40 bottles of men's cologne. A filigreed framed photograph of a smiling fair-haired high school girl dressed in a low-cut prom frock glared from among the swanky, meticulously arranged bottles, a pink carnation the size of a cantaloupe pinned to her breast.

My side of the room was furnished with a metal bed frame and stained mattress, a sturdy wood chair, a utilitarian dresser and a desk—boxy, indestructible furniture topped with blond Formica.

"You must be Carl," my father said, grabbing the kid's hand firmly and shaking it.

"Gosh," Carl replied, stunned perhaps by the bluntness of my father's introduction and the realization that a stranger knew his name. "Good to meet you," he continued. "I'm sorry my parents aren't here; they had to head back an hour ago." Carl was doing his best to be gracious, an anxious smile plastered on his thin, pink face.

In early August, I'd received a letter from Elon's housing office containing the name and address of my assigned roommate so that I could get in touch with him, but I hadn't bothered to write Carl, and I hadn't heard a word from him.

"Well, Carl," my father said, "it's certainly good to finally meet you." And he set about ascertaining Carl's census information, asking three or four probing questions. Within five minutes, he'd collected my roommate's entire history—date of birth, his mother's maiden name, his father's occupation, his home address in the DC suburbs of Northern Virginia, and the number of siblings in the family. "What do you plan to study at college?" my father asked.

"I'm going to be a German major," he said, proudly.

Somewhere in my brief, disastrous encounter with foreign languages, I learned where the past participle form of a verb appears in a German sentence. If Carl could speak German, even a little bit, he had to be a whole lot brainier than I was, since I wasn't sure where the past participle form of a verb appeared in an English sentence.

Meanwhile, my mother and I haphazardly stuffed underwear, T-shirts and socks into empty drawers. I'd signed up for the college linen service, but we'd packed a set of sheets in case the service wasn't available when we arrived. We made up my bed, stretching the sheets taut between us and tucking in the corners of my father's brown World War II Navy blanket as a bedspread. My side of the room was nowhere as elegant as Carl's, but it projected, I thought, an austere, unpretentious quality.

"Sure do have a lot of bottles of perfume," my father continued in a gently reproachful tone. His use of the term "perfume" was intentional. He was in the habit of identifying the people he met as types—the criminal, the jerk, the queer, the bum, etc.—and he wasn't fond of men who wore too much "perfume." He called them sissies or, if he was in a particularly bad mood, simps, wimps, or pissants. My father considered every male a homosexual until he proved himself otherwise.

"I collect colognes," Carl explained proudly, tumbling headlong into my father's trap. "It's a hobby." He went on to enumerate the virtues of various bouquets, uncapping two or three bottles and allowing my father to take a reluctant whiff.

"Very nice. I like that one," my father said. I could taste the sarcasm.

With my shirts and trousers safely stowed away in the double closet and high bureau, we sat around for a few minutes discussing the humid weather and the bad road between Henderson and Durham. Finally, my father got a squirrely look in his eye that signaled it was time to head home.

"We've got another nine hours to drive," he said, exaggerating. "We'd better get started." He shook my hand.

My father was a stickler about masculine gestures, insisting that I look him directly in the eye when our hands were firmly clasped, which I did. Now he averted his eyes, whether out of consternation or despair I couldn't determine. "Keep your nose clean," he said, offering in one concise sentence his most profound advice. Then he handed me a ten-dollar bill. "This has got to last you the rest of the month. You won't get any more money until October first."

My father had stipulated that I would receive an allowance of twenty-five dollars a month, which was a pittance. Out of that monthly check, I had to pay to wash my clothes, purchase supplies—pens, paper, soap, shampoo, snacks, and an occasional mug of beer—and I had to save a few dollars for rides home at Thanksgiving and Christmas. If by some miracle, I happened to get a date, I'd have to find a more generous source of cash. But I was thankful for every cent and said so. My mother hugged me and gave me a parting peck on the cheek. Then my parents slipped quickly out the door and down the hall.

That's when I remembered my Rolling Stones album left in the back seat of the car. I hurried to the stairwell and yanked open the door in time to hear my father's voice echo upward: "I guarantee you he'll be home before Thanksgiving and in basic training by spring."

They hadn't seen me. I allowed the door to drift shut.

My father's prediction was perfectly in keeping with his pessimistic temperament. Even if I hadn't overheard him, I would have known that's how he felt about my chances of succeeding in college. He always prophesied doom and gloom, especially regarding my future. "Do you think you'll ever amount to anything?" he was fond of asking.

"Well, I haven't so far," I'd always answer.

I had no idea how my first semester might unfold, and my father had no way of knowing if I would rise to the occasion, but he was perfectly willing to forecast that I'd come whining home within a month or two. As for basic training, if anything kept me in college, it was the threat of having to play grabass under a sweltering Georgia sun. I wasn't angry or possessed of a need to prove him wrong. I accepted his lack of faith as typical. To hell with the Stones. I'd heard enough pop music in my first few minutes in Smith dorm to keep me jiving for the next ten years, so I strolled to the window at the far end of the second floor and watched as the Fairlane pulled up to the brick gateway. The brake lights flashed red. I held my breath. The lights went dark, the Ford turned left onto Haggard Avenue, windshield wipers flapping in the drizzle, and disappeared. My parents were gone. I was emancipated.

• • •

Back in my room I collapsed on my lumpy mattress, still sculpted to the physical imperfections of a multitude of previous occupants, to contemplate my newfound freedom. My God, it was exhilarating! I closed my eyes and allowed my mind to go blank. All the tension drained from my body, and I enjoyed a few blessed breaths of liberation. My old life—all eighteen years of accumulated absurdity—was clearly behind me. I was a blank slate.

It was Carl who jarred me back into the sensible world. "Have you picked up your packet?" he asked. He was still arranging bottles of cologne on his dresser. "They have them over in the Alamance Building. You'll need to get your room key and a schedule of events."

"Oh, yeah," I said, and sat up on the edge of the bed. "I was just about to head over there." My parents had been absent from my life for ten minutes, and here was a complete stranger reminding me that there were responsibilities that needed my immediate attention. It was annoying. Who was this guy, and why was he *my* roommate?

Unfortunately, he was correct. I needed to get a grasp on what would be occupying my time for the next week, so I went clambering down the stairwell, out the side door, and under the colonnades to the east entrance of the Alamance Building. Folding tables were set up in the rotunda, and fretful parents and their progeny were in line to collect their packets. As I approached the sign-in table, a burly, butch-headed upperclassman slapped an idiotic purple and gold flannel beanie on my head. "You must wear this at all times," he said, explaining that I couldn't, under penalty of death, step on the big E set in tile at the entrance to the Mooney Building, wherever that was. Such monumental transgressions, he explained, were considered extremely bad form and might result in something unpleasant hitting the fan.

I swiped the beanie off my head and examined it. It was mortifying. Stupid. And I resolved then and there not to wear the damn thing unless threatened with expulsion from college, immediate induction into the military or physical injury. I hadn't worn any sort of head covering since the blessed demise of the Davy Crockett raccoon-cap craze. A hand slammed down on the back of my neck and someone blurted: "Get that beanie back on your head freshman, and keep it there!" And that's what I did.

I was intent on checking out the female talent, but there was too much commotion to focus on the girls in attendance. Upperclassmen had been quick to pin the lookers to the wall while explaining in whispers the necessity of wearing a beanie. "You'll look so cute in this," I heard one of them say. "What dorm are you staying in?"

No purpose was served in hanging around, so I grabbed my packet and hurried back to the safety of my room where I found Carl arranging his shoes alphabetically by brand, aligned heel to heel, on his side of the closet—Converse All Stars, Florsheim, Hush Puppies, Top-Siders. I removed the "Schedule of Events" from my packet and gave it the once over: "6:00 p.m.—Picnic—South of McEwen, 7:30 p.m. Assembly—Whitley Auditorium, 8 p.m.—[visit] Faculty Homes." The program cover contained an emphatic directive: "ALL FRESHMEN are required to be present for this entire program" and then in smaller type: "Please keep this program with you throughout the entire week."

Of the functions listed for Saturday and Sunday, I figured I'd make the picnic—hot dogs and hamburgers were on my list—but I already knew I'd be absent from most of the other events. I understood how college worked. If I didn't show up for every program, who'd know? Would some toady be hanging out at freshman gatherings to write down the names of the slackers who weren't present? It wasn't likely, and I was willing to take my chances. Years of living under a quasi-military regime had instilled in me a healthy disdain for authority.

At 5 o'clock, Carl and I walked over to McEwen Dining Hall. He continued to yammer about the German courses he intended to ace. (Did little Elon College even offer German? I couldn't recall reading descriptions for such courses in the catalog.)

"I'm going to make German my major so I can get a job with the State Department," he said, matter-of-factly. I kept my mouth shut; I had no idea what I'd be doing in the next five minutes.

The drizzle, a steady warmish spray that frizzed my hair and wilted my starched shirt, had resumed, and the picnic, which was to be held under the trees in front of McEwen, was a bust. We ate inside, queuing up to have our food served by the cafeteria staff. Unfortunately, there was little of the socializing the outdoor gathering was intended to encourage. The girls sat on one side of the room, the boys on the other, as if we were eighth graders at our first school dance.

After supper, Carl hustled off to Whitley Auditorium to take in the administration's policies regarding the state of the world, and I moseyed on back to our room to give the "Schedule of Events" a closer look. When I stepped from the stairwell onto the second floor, the hall was blessedly quiet. Apparently, I was the only delinquent. I kicked back on my bunk and began reading where I'd stopped a few days before in *The Brinkmanship of Galahad Threepwood*. If I needed reassurance that the world was utterly banal, Wodehouse was my man.

Carl strolled in at nine to inform me that I'd "missed out on some important stuff."

"Like what?" I asked.

"You know, going to class and taking notes and other stuff like that."

I knew I could learn all there was to know concerning college life by chatting with a competent sophomore for five minutes. I'd sat in on numerous bull sessions with friends who'd completed their freshman year, so I didn't feel the need to ask any probing questions.

Carl donned a pair of pajamas. Jesus, this guy actually owned matching PJ tops and shorty bottoms; I was sprawled on my bed in my boxer shorts and a T-shirt. Once appropriately attired, he hurried off to the bathroom with a towel, a bar of soap, a tube of toothpaste, a toothbrush and a bottle of mouthwash, leaving me to read my paperback.

When he returned, the room was aromatic with his minty fresh breath, and his smiling face was shiny clean in the glow from the overhead light, which he switched off, even though I was still reading. Carl crawled into his bunk and I slipped between the sheets on my side of the room. For a minute or two there was silence. Then a voice asked, "What's your major?"

I considered feigning sleep, but answered reluctantly, "I have no idea."

Unfortunately, Carl was the loquacious sort. He was going to sign up for physics and run for class president in addition to majoring in German. Then he started in on his personal life. I had no choice but to lie there in the dark and listen to him brag about his girlfriend, who was a freshman at a college in Virginia, and how they were going to get married before the year was out, a notion that struck me as utterly demented. "We love each other very, very much," he declared without a trace of embarrassment. "We're meant for each other. Do you have a girlfriend back in Annapolis?"

A lie would have only prolonged the conversation, so I fessed up. "No."

"My girlfriend's picture is on my desk," he said. "Take a look at her tomorrow. She looks like Brigitte Bardot. We've been going steady for three years."

"Three years?" I couldn't conceive of dating one girl for three years, even a Brigitte Bardot look-alike, even Bardot herself. I tended to get sick to death of people, male or female, in five minutes, and Carl had already exceeded his time limit.

"Yeah, well, neither of us has ever been attracted to anyone else," he continued, "so we might as well get married. Why wait?"

"I see your point," I said.

"As soon as I'm elected class president, I'll have her move down here, and we'll get a place off campus."

"Gosh, that would be great," I said, and meant it.

"So, you don't have any ideas about a major?" he asked, again.

I wanted to tell him that I was intent on staying out of the army and away from Vietnam and that I'd take whatever courses would accomplish those objectives. Otherwise, I intended to drink beer and find a woman who wanted to go dancing. My immediate plans were no more or less complicated than that.

"No," I said again.

"I'll think we'll make good roommates," he said, pausing for emphasis. "My guess is you'll find me something of a perfectionist. I like things just so. You might have noticed that I like organization, you know, my colognes, shirts, and shoes."

"I noticed," I said.

"And you'll find that I'm pretty strict about my study habits. I have to put myself on a schedule to produce the level of work that I'm capable of, and that requires self-discipline." He paused. "I'm the first to admit that I didn't work up to my full potential in high school, but this is a new beginning for me, a new start, and I intend to take full advantage of the opportunity."

All I wanted was a little sleep; I'd been up since 5:30 a.m., and I was flat worn out.

"I'll tell you something else," he continued. "If I *weren't* in college, I'd be a marine. I'm joining up as soon as I graduate."

This absurd pronouncement was mildly unnerving. "You *want* to join the Marines?" I asked.

"Oh, yeah. I'll be an officer, of course, but I plan on joining up. *Semper fi*."

Except for my friend Barrie Barnes, whose father had forced him to join the military, none of my high school friends considered the service an appealing alternative to attending college or doing nothing. The war was an abstraction fought by guys who couldn't go to college, and South Vietnam, a mysterious country on the other side of the planet, wasn't a threat to anyone but itself. I thought about telling him that I had better things to do with my life than sloshing through rice paddies and sitting in a ditch waiting to have my head blown off, but I kept my mouth shut. I was sick of discussing the war.

"After I leave the service," Carl continued, "I plan on taking the Civil Service test for the State Department so that I can . . ."

There's no telling how long Carl's monologue continued. Lying there in the humid Carolina dark, I reminded myself that I was, as Grandmother Drager put it, "one of a million" college freshmen experiencing their first night away from home. Probably most of them were homesick and considering packing up and heading back to mommy and daddy. I was perfectly happy where I was, and I certainly wasn't looking for an argument with anyone, especially my new roommate. I had to live with this guy for the next nine months, but I didn't have to be his best friend. Happenstance had thrown us together in this tiny room on the second floor of a dormitory at an obscure college in the wilds of Carolina, and there wasn't a damn thing I could do about that.

If Carl had gone on to explicate his sex life in detail—the bosomy chick in the photograph was rather fetching—I might have listened, but he didn't, and I dozed off.

# Three

Nothing in my life was ever easier than making friends in Smith dorm. With the doors open to most rooms, inmates circulated freely during those first few days, introducing themselves by simply contributing a story or joke to an ongoing conversation. I met Scott Roberson, a lean, dark-haired baseball player from outside Richmond; Gene Matthews, a Deep South Southerner who billed himself as a "lean mean dancing machine"; curly-headed Witt Halle from New York state, a quiet guy who nonetheless contributed an occasional sour joke; Steve Maynard, a smiling, good-natured goof who walked like a penguin and was capable of an occasional zinger. And most importantly, I met Steve Tindall from Wilmington, Delaware.

Tindall (that's what we called him immediately) simply marched into our conversation, extended his hand, and introduced himself. He came from a background not unlike my own. In the summers he'd worked at Rehoboth Beach, Delaware, the little seaside town where my sainted maternal grandparents had often taken me to stay at the mildewy Pennsylvania Railroad House. Slightly taller than I and sporting the shaggiest hair of any freshman, he had a masterful recall of minutiae from popular culture, which he employed to good effect in his humor. We'd grown up with the same TV programs—*Captain Video and His Video Rangers, Andy's Gang, Sky King, Crusader Rabbit and Rags the Tiger, Mr. District Attorney.* He excelled at mimicry and could do a masterful imitation of Walter Cronkite's closing from *You Are There*, a popular TV program that had aired in the early '50s: "What sort of day was it? A day like all days...." He also had an intense interest in music, especially jug band music and the blues. The guy owned a Big Bill Broonzy album and a cheap mandolin.

In thirty minutes, I'd met the guys who'd be my closest friends for the next nine months. And by Sunday at lunch, we began to take our meals together. We strutted over to McEwen and moaned and groaned over the food, which wasn't all that bad—a trifle starchy but adequate—and we repeated the obligatory urban myth concerning doses of saltpeter sprinkled in the mashed potatoes to make it impossible for the male students to impregnate unwitting co-eds, as if such an opportunity might present itself.

• • •

On September 12 and 13, the Piedmont was waterlogged by the remnants of Hurricane Betsy, a category four storm that ravaged the Gulf Coast and then drifted into the Carolinas, where it stalled, dumping three inches of rain on the campus. The steam pipes that ran to the dorms were being replaced, and the ubiquitous red clay was transformed into a sticky adhesive that was impossible to shed. It coated the walkways and marked the path of every student who entered or left a campus building. The goo clung to my shoes and somehow migrated onto the cuffs of my khaki trousers, leaving a burgundy stain that wouldn't wash out.

On Monday night we were scheduled to attend a YMCA party at the north side of the Alamance Building, a gathering I'd scratched off my list of to-dos. There was a guy on the hall from Burlington—we'd nicknamed him "Townie"—who had a car, and he and a few of his buds announced that they were going to Ritchie's Tap Room, a beer joint on South Church Street. "We're gonna get us some Blue Ribbon," one of them blurted. "You wanna come along? Beer's a quarter."

"You're going to do what?" I asked.

"Get us some beer," he said again. "Y'all can get yourself a mug for twenty-five cent."

This was the first example of obscure Southernese I'd encountered. Forget "y'all" and the dropped g's on -ing words and other clichéd usages like "Y'all come back and see us now." It occurred to me that the uniqueness of Southern speech exists in syntax, such as "We're going to get *us* some. . . ." The extra "us" used for possession seemed redundant. And then there was the dropping of "s" on "cents," as in "I've got me twenty-five cent."

The invitation was a good chance to escape the dorm and drink beer with a few local guys who knew the ropes, so Carl and I rode into town with the Burlington boys.

We parked behind the Tap Room, a tiny cinderblock cubicle—probably an erstwhile Tastee Freez—with an obliquely angled picture window overlooking a funeral home. Five booths lined the wall. A restroom with a white metal towel dispenser manufactured in Toledo, Ohio hung over a filthy commode crammed into a closet at the back of the room. The proceedings were overseen by a rotund bald bartender named "Shorty" who served up a frosty mug of draft beer and a pink pickled egg with saltines for thirty-five cents. A couple of my new Burlington friends drank a stomach-churning concoction called "red-eye," a draft beer mixed with tomato juice with salt and pepper sprinkled into the foam. After a brew or two, we engaged in sophisticated freshman repartee, composed primarily of bad jokes and outright lies. The Tap Room would become a regular Friday and Saturday night destination for freshman guys with nothing better to do, a sad assemblage of forlorn souls that would too often include me.

On Tuesday night, the college sponsored a dance. Listed in the orientation program as a "social hour," it was an obvious misnomer since it was scheduled from 8:30 to 11:00. The informal gathering was to be held on the second floor of McEwen Dining Hall, and only freshmen were allowed to attend. I was glad about that. If upperclassmen were present, I stood little chance of meeting a willing dance partner.

Of our little band of miscreants, only Tindall, Scott, Gene, and I attended the dance. Carl, by way of preparing himself for a job with the State Department, had begun to frequent the Tap Room daily, and Steve Maynard was no dancer, so the four of us wandered over to McEwen to inspect the available female population.

The lights on the second-floor dance hall were adequately dimmed, and the Monzas, a local band who had a regional hit with "Hey! I Know You," played their sanitized version of soul music. The plump female singer and her partner set the tone for the evening by dancing what was called "the Shag," a cross between a minuet and a '40s jitterbug.

I had come prepared to do the Annapolis bop, but I could see that free-form gyrations were inappropriate in my new environment. I realized, too, that there was no faking the steps these Southern guys were putting down. "What kind of dance is that, and how do you do it?" I asked Gene. He kindly pointed out the essential moves while we stood with the other pimply forlorn stags milling in a dark corner of the room.

"Watch her," Gene said as "Sixty Minute Man" neared its conclusion. "She'll do a belly roll." I stared as the band's singer glided through her stylized shuffle and then performed a mildly sexual redistribution of her belly fat that produced an illusion whereby she rolled up and onto the male dancer's stomach. "That's it," Gene said. "That's a belly roll!" I was impressed.

In addition to a working knowledge of the Shag and a familiarity with the accompanying music, I could see it was essential to dress the part if you wanted to be known as a Southern guy who had a way with the ladies. I'd later hear this variety of Southern male referred to as Shag Boy, Diddly-Bopper, Basic Dude, Strander Man and other less flattering genera, but one thing was certain: His sole purpose in life was to dance, and he knew exactly what he was doing.

What immediately irritated me about the Shag Boy was his coiffure. My hair was hopelessly curly. When it rained, it exploded into a Don King 'do. The Shag Boy had perfect hair. His light brown to blondish mane was cut in a layered pageboy that was amazingly frizz-resistant and drifted lackadaisically across his blemish-free forehead. He usually wore a red, green or dark blue alpaca sweater over a starched white Oxford cloth button-down shirt cursively monogrammed on the collar and cuffs. In some cases, the sweater was tucked into his houndstooth, high-waisted trousers. A shiny alligator belt transected him like a sugar bag.

But it was the Shag Boy's feet that most attracted my attention. He was wearing black leather loafers with a fancy tonguelike flap from which protruded two tassels. These strange shoes struck me as a trifle effeminate, but they were obviously an obligatory accessory. I noticed that Gene was wearing the same style of footwear, and I asked, "What kind of shoes are those?"

"They're Nettletons," he said. "If you want to dance the Shag, you've got to have a pair of Nettletons."

"How much do these Nettletons cost?" I asked.

"You can buy a pair at Younts-DeBoe in Greensboro for $30," Gene said.

The mere mention of Greensboro, home of the largest all-female university in the United States, was heartening, but $30 was beyond my immediate means. Nettletons were, I thought, flat-out ugly, but if such accessories were a requirement for a regular palooka like myself to meet girls, I'd have to own a pair.

Still, I didn't have a clue how to dance the Shag. But I was determined to try my luck with my Annapolis steps. Once these Southerners saw the moves I put down, they'd make the adjustments. Soon everyone in the South would be dancing like they were native Annapolitans.

A bevy of likely females was huddled on the far side of the room, as if they were at a mandatory junior high sock hop, earnestly confabbing among themselves. It remained for me to choose a likely partner. I focused on a cute little brunette, her neck-length hair curled in a flip with wispy bangs brushing her forehead. She was enticing in a white blouse with a "virgin pin," a chrome circle attached to the left side of her Peter Pan collar, a purely symbolic adornment that conveyed no factual import, and was otherwise neatly attired in a blue pleated skirt and navy Pappagallo flats. Her moonish face was graced with an easy smile that suggested a modicum of compassion. I couldn't make out the color of her eyes, but they were unusually round and outlined in thickly applied mascara. Her nose, tiny and white, glowed between clownishly rouged cheeks.

"Go ahead, ask her to dance," Gene suggested, nodding toward the object of my attention.

"Do you think she'll dance with me?" I asked.

"It's not likely," he answered, with uncommon prescience.

I stepped out anyway, strutting boldly across the dance floor, displaying an enviable élan, and confronted the startled girl, whose face instantly blanched. "Would you like to dance?" I asked with a reassuring measure of savoir faire.

She didn't smile but nodded in utter bewilderment. Her friends, each dressed in matching Villager outfits, looked me up and down. I gently took her hand in mine and led her to the center of the dance floor. If I was in and in for good, I was going to give it my best shot, and as the band cranked up a cover of the Temps' "My Girl," I began to put down my super-cool Annapolis step— my feet spread shoulder width, knees slightly bent and my hands extended at waist height. I smiled at my partner. She stared back— and stood stark still, arms straight by her sides. Then she spoke in a voice barely audible above the music. "I don't know how to dance like that," she said, and bolted, disappearing into her gaggle of friends, who continued to stare at me, a look of abject horror on their pink faces.

I stood alone in the middle of the dance floor, a shiver of disbelief quivering through my bones. It occurred to me that my prospective dance partner had made a terrible mistake. She'd probably come gushing back to me, laughing at the silly joke she'd played. "I'm fooling," she'd say. "I can't wait to dance with you." But that didn't happen, and I was left alone with every face in the room staring at me.

With what dignity I could muster, I slinked back to the dark corner where my new friends waited. I looked questioningly at Gene, who was smiling broadly. "I told you she wouldn't dance with you," he said.

"She didn't even give me a chance."

"Shot down," Tindall observed, chuckling. Scott, who must have sensed my embarrassment, remained silent.

"She knew the minute you took her hand that you didn't know

what you were doing," Gene said.

"How could she tell that?"

"If you don't hold her hand in the right way," he said, "she's not going to dance with you. It's that simple."

It occurred to me that I had a lot to learn if I was going to be a cool cat in the Carolinas.

• • •

When upperclassmen returned to campus, it quickly became apparent there were student coteries other than the Shag Boy and his female complement. Members of fraternities and sororities were the most obvious with their boisterous camaraderie and arrogant detachment. And there was a tight-knit crowd of beatnik-like students who were members of the Liberal Arts Forum, aloof intellectuals who sponsored academic lectures and cogitated on subjects too esoteric for the freshman mind. When they passed each other in the hallway, they clicked their tongues in greeting, an exclusionary gesture that struck me as amusing. The tongue clicker who clicked first produced a deep resonant cluck, and the respondent pitched his or her click slighter higher, an acknowledgment of one's social standing among the bohemians.

On the evening of Thursday, September 16, I attended a hootenanny in West Residence Hall, the largest of the girls' dorms on campus. The lobby was furnished with velvet-covered Victorian chairs and sofas, and I sat around listening to a long-haired sophomore play his Martin guitar and sing Kingston Trio tunes.

As we all sang "Goodnight, Irene" or some equally sanitized folk song, I wondered what my friends in Annapolis were doing. I'd been in college for a week, and my old life was already a thickening fog of football Fridays and high school dances. I thought of my former coworkers at the Safeway banging on their cash registers and busily restocking shelves. At home my mother was probably arguing with my sister about her latest bad-news boyfriend, and my brother was chowing down on a bowl of Cap'n Crunch and watching *Batman*. My father would be stretched out on the sofa in his boxer shorts awaiting the collect phone call in which I begged him to rescue me from the horrors of college life. It was lights out for my friend Barrie Barnes, who was, at that instant, suffering through basic training. Tomorrow he'd be bugled awake at 5 a.m. for a ten-mile hike and other abject physical torments.

    I was lucky, and I knew it.

# Four

Wide awake at 6 a.m. on the first day of fall semester classes, I took a quick shower and donned my best camouflage—a pair of khakis, a freshly laundered white shirt, my mud-stained loafers—and hurried under an ashen sky to McEwen to gobble down a big breakfast of scrambled eggs, sausages, and lumpy grits. I drank a cup of weak Lipton tea dosed with five packets of pure cane sugar and hurried back to my room to gather my textbooks.

    Carl had stumbled in about 1:30 a.m. the night before and collapsed face down, fully clothed, into his unmade bed. While I was chowing down at breakfast, he'd slipped off one of his Hush Puppies and shed his red plaid shirt, which lay crumpled in an ever-growing pile of dirty laundry on his desktop. Now he was snoring fitfully, the sheet pulled over his head, one bony foot protruding from beneath his chenille spread, an arm dangling over the edge of the bed frame. I knew he had an 8 o'clock class.

    "Carl, don't you need to get ready for class?" I asked, patting him gently on the shoulder.

    "Go away," grumbled the lovesick German major who aspired to become class president but who'd failed to have his name entered on the ballot in the recent campus election. He smelled of the Tap

Room: fusty cigarette butts and stale Blue Ribbon.

"You'll miss your 8 o'clock," I reminded him.

"Screw it," he mumbled.

Before leaving the room, I stared at my reflection in the dresser mirror and willed the frizziness out of my hair. The oppressive humidity had worked havoc on my curls, and a stiff brushing accomplished nothing. I plopped my obnoxious beanie on the top of my head so that it covered most of the offending ringlets. I grabbed my English textbooks, picked up a new spiral notepad, and carefully inserted two fresh BIC pens in my shirt pocket.

The only problem with being mildly compulsive is that I was always early, and as I stepped from my room, I noticed the hall was empty. "Goin' Out of My Head" droned from someone's clock radio at the far end of the empty passway.

Once inside the empty Alamance Building, I noticed that the empty echoic first-floor hallway was paved with randomly broken white terra-cotta tiles set in glossy concrete worn smooth. My footfalls reverberated upward as I ascended the stairwell to the second floor. Since I was the first English 111 student to set foot in room 207 that morning, I spent a minute or two marveling at the ancient brass toggle switch that electrified the opaque globes dangling from chains through which were woven cloth-wrapped wires. When I flipped the switch, the dim artificial light did little to illuminate the room and only slightly augmented the muted pastel glow from the wavy greenish-glass windows that lined the outer wall. Rather than the fiberglass and Formica one-piece desks I'd grown accustomed to in high school, the room was furnished with ancient cast-iron frames supporting wooden pew-like benches with wobbly L-shaped writing surfaces. The room smelled vaguely of mildew and sweat.

I selected what I thought was an inconspicuous seat halfway

down the center aisle, where it was likely the benches in front and behind me would fill with eager faces. I opened my notebook and wrote at the top of the first page in my best barely decipherable cursive: *English 111, Friday, September 17, 1965.*

I'd given my opening foray into the rigors of academe considerable thought, and I intended to coast through my first class session by being invisible, thus the white shirt and khaki pants I'd donned earlier. If I looked like every other male freshman, perhaps the professor wouldn't notice me. I believed that a few of my less sophisticated peers would cooperate by wearing Madras or paisley shirts or other brightly colored garments that would divert attention from me and onto them. As a second line of defense, I intended to make myself disappear by collapsing inward like a deflating balloon, a trick of mind over matter whereby I became a part of the floor, walls and ceiling. If that didn't work, I intended to take copious notes, focusing unwaveringly on the task of writing down every inspirational word the professor uttered. If he or she were to ask me a direct question, I'd keep my eyes riveted on my notebook and scribble like a madman.

Ten minutes after I'd staked out the most inconspicuous seat in the room, I was still the only student present, and I felt a trifle ridiculous for having shown up so early. Good Lord, it was only 7:30 a.m.! So I turned in my catalog to the course description and read for the umpteenth time a bunch of gobbledygook concerning grammatical fundamentals and mechanics, "with an emphasis on the student writing." Then I leafed through my *Harbrace College Handbook*, pausing to stare blankly at a mysterious chapter on something called subjunctive mood.

At 7:45 a.m. the other freshmen began to arrive, warily easing into the room and selecting seats along the wall and in the back of the class. The sophomores were less timid. They were repeating the course and greeted each other by name, occupying seats close to the rear door where they immediately began speculating as to who the professor might be (in those days, the class schedule didn't identify who would teach the class; you signed up and took your chances). The freshmen were hesitant, solitary, flat-out scared half to death. And of course we were wearing those stupid maroon and gold beanies.

By 8:05 a.m. the commotion in the hall had abated, but our professor had yet to make his or her entrance. The sophomores groused among themselves. I sat as still as possible, staring at the school clock hanging above the blackboard—8:10, 8:15, 8:20. How long were we required to wait for a professor? I'd heard that it was ten minutes for a Ph.D. and five for a master's. Maybe the professor had two Ph.Ds. Or maybe I was in the wrong room? I checked my schedule: "Room 207" was printed next to the course title.

At 8:25 a.m., the door at the front of the classroom burst open and in strutted a thin, thirty-ish man of above average height. His thick slicked-back dark brown hair was neatly combed, and a cultivated Hitleresque cowlick drifted across the left side of his forehead and onto his right eyebrow. He was nattily attired in a well-worn gray suit, white shirt and skewed black bow tie. A glowing unfiltered cigarette dangled precariously between his index and middle fingers. He dropped his leather portfolio briefcase, worn ocher at the corners and seams, heavily on the desk, adeptly unbuckled the flap, withdrew a pile of books and let them drop onto the desktop with a startling clap.

After giving our anxious faces a quick once over, he strolled to the nearest window—his walk was fluid, catlike, creepy—and pushed up the sash with a dusty rattle. He stared distractedly into the overcast sky, focusing on some invisible point on the distant horizon. And that's when the sophomores bolted. They vanished almost soundlessly, as if they were executing an oft-rehearsed drill. I assumed they were on their way to the registrar's office to drop the course. "It's Reed," I heard one of them murmur from the hallway.

My God, this was the infamous Tully Reed, a professor whose name had been mentioned only in hushed, derogatory tones since I'd set foot on campus. "Pray you don't get Reed for freshman English," I'd overheard an upperclassman say while standing in line at registration.

With the sophomores gone, only eight freshmen remained in the room. I pretended to be reading in my *Harbrace*, all the while keeping a wary eye on the malevolent stranger who had intruded into my life. He took a final deep drag on his cigarette, propelled the glowing butt out the window with a flick of his forefinger, and sauntered back to his desk. He paused to survey the class again, a scowl of abject contempt on his face. His eyes were dark and piercing, his expression drawn, the skin tight against his thickset jaw and high cheekbones. Without warning, he pointed randomly into the group of terrified students and asked in a commanding voice, "What is Indo-European?"

My heart stopped. For a breathless instant I was convinced he was addressing me. When I realized he'd singled out the unfortunate female student one row up and to the left, I stared intently at my Weejuns, lest his gaze slip sidewise and our eyes lock momentarily. In my peripheral vision, I could see the victim's eyes widen and the blood drain from her scared-pale face. She said nothing for ten seconds, and then Reed began searching the room for a more responsive quarry. Sweet Jesus, I prayed, don't let him pick me! I hadn't the faintest idea what Indo-European was.

"Well-ah-umm-ah," the quivering girl stammered. "I don't know, sir."

"Do you know why you don't know?" Reed asked. He didn't wait for an answer. "It's because you're ignorant." He smiled for dramatic effect and then continued. "When this semester is over—if you make it through the semester—you won't be nearly as ignorant as you are right now. I can assure you of that."

As tears welled in the girl's eyes, I felt myself free-falling into the dark, unfathomable void that exists beyond absolute desperation. I hunched my shoulders inward, decreasing my profile, and slumped down in my seat, pressing my chin to my chest. What if he asked me to spell an ordinary word that any fourth grader could spell (I had somehow missed out on phonics in elementary school), something simple like "separate"?—which I had a habit of spelling with three e's. "You," he might say, pointing his index finger directly between my eyes. "Yeah, you. How do you spell separate?"

If that happened and Reed ridiculed me in front of my peers— "Look," he might say, singling me out, "this imbecile can't spell a simple three-syllable word"—my college career would be over. I'd be a goner. I'd slink back to my dorm room in disgrace, pack up my belongings and phone home with the news of my failure, fulfilling my father's prophecy. I'd get drafted and end up in a ditch in Asia. I might be killed, all because a smartass college professor asked me to spell a word I should have learned in elementary school.

But he didn't ask another question. Instead, he addressed the entire class: "I'm Tully Reed, acting chairman of the English Department, and you should all sign up for this course again next semester. Most freshmen fail my English 111." Then he outlined what he expected from us during the coming weeks. I took a deep breath and scribbled down every syllable.

First, we were required to buy three texts—a powder-blue edition of the *Harbrace College Handbook*, which I'd already purchased, a paperback copy of Edith Hamilton's *Mythology*, and a volume of essays to serve as models for our writing.

"Make sure you have these texts with you by class on Monday," Reed ordered. "Now, the course requirements. They're simple enough for even freshmen to remember. You'll write four essays, and I'll grade them, and then we'll have a final exam, which will also be an essay. You'll need to demonstrate proficiency in audience analysis, topic selection and thesis support. You'll lose one letter grade for each grammar, spelling or punctuation error you make. Five mistakes and you've earned an F. Is that understood?" He paused again as if he expected us to respond "Yes, sir" in unison. When no one spoke, he continued, "I'll average all the grades, and you'll receive exactly what you've earned, which in most cases will be an F."

That's when I realized that Tully Reed wasn't going to teach us how to write. There would be no gradual demystification of the subject matter, no startling insights into the art of argument and exposition. We weren't going to *learn* how to write; we were going to *prove* we could write—or we'd flunk out on our butts.

After five more minutes of condemning us to a lifetime of failure, Reed began to speak his mind, discoursing briefly on the myriad injustices of the war in Vietnam. Propped on the edge of his desk, he brushed back his cowlick and paused to gather his thoughts. "Our country is headed down a dangerous road," he began and went on to characterize the draft as "iniquitous"—I spelled it "innickious" in my notes—snatching up the poor and ignorant and forcing them to fight and die in a faraway country that could not survive save as a puppet of the United States government. We were squandering our treasure and wasting the lives of our young men. "If you were a Negro," he said, pointing at me, "you'd be in the army now and not sitting in some comfy college classroom. You'd be somewhere in Southeast Asia wading through a rice paddy. Either that or you'd be in a body bag headed home to your mama." On and on he went, enumerating Lyndon Johnson's countless transgressions and the absurdity of war.

I don't know how the other students reacted to Reed's uninvited tirade—they had sense enough to keep their mouths shut—but this much I was sure of: He was wasting his time convincing me that the war was wrong. I was singing first soprano in the choir.

At 8:45, Reed dismissed the class—"Get out of here," he said—and I slipped quickly from the room and into the hallway. As I descended the stairs to the first floor, I considered withdrawing from the course and picking up a more amiable professor, a kindhearted soul who'd sympathize with a desperate freshman who was unsure of his writing skills and couldn't spell worth a damn. But I decided not to drop Reed's class when I caught a glimpse of the long line of students in front of the registrar's office. Coping with this Reed guy had to be easier, at least for the time being, than standing in line for two hours only to discover that the courses taught by the easygoing professors were closed out. As always with my younger self, indolence trumped judgment.

I had an hour break between classes and strolled back to the dorm, overjoyed to be free of Tully Reed for the time being. Most of the doors on second Smith were open, and a cacophony of pop music boomed down the hall—a worrisome mingling of "Stop! In the Name of Love" by the Supremes and "Eve of Destruction" by Barry McGuire—brushing against me as I hurried to my room, where I discovered Carl lying flat on his belly, the sheet still pulled over his head. I touched his shoulder again, as much to aggravate him as to awaken him, and asked, "Don't you have a 10 o'clock class?" He pulled up the covers tighter and grunted. He was going nowhere, so I let him be. I dropped my books on my desk and stretched out on my bed to review Reed's intimidating performance. A sick, fretful uneasiness churned deep in the pit of my stomach. English 111 was not an auspicious beginning to my college career.

At 9:50 a.m., I returned to the second floor of Alamance for Durward Stokes' History of Western Civilization. Stokes was my advisor, so I already liked the guy. I'd heard via the student grapevine that he'd once owned a hardware store in Graham, the town east of Burlington. When he retired, he'd enrolled at Elon—he must have been well into his fifties at the time—and completed his undergraduate degree and matriculated at UNC-Chapel Hill to take his master's and Ph.D. in history. If I was looking for a kindly professor, Stokes fit the bill, an upright Southern gentleman with a deeply etched, square-chinned face, pouchy eyes, and graying hair. He lectured through narrative, which he wielded with the grace of any good Southern storyteller. His was, thank goodness, a welcome reprieve from the ranting of Tully Reed. There wasn't a trace of arrogance in Dr. Stokes' genial countenance.

After Western Civilization, I hurried to the Mooney Building to make my way to W.W. Sloan's Survey of the Old Testament. A line of students trailed up the side staircase to the second story of the building with the forbidden E set in terra-cotta on the first-floor entrance. The campus was now crowded with upperclassmen, and they had brought with them a welcoming air of self-confidence. They were survivors, they knew the system, and they joked among themselves as they inched upward, chatting and laughing. Their presence re-established the pecking order that normally existed on campus. With a goofy maroon and gold beanie perched on my skull, I felt like the freshman dorm rat I was.

W.W. Sloan was a diminutive scoliotic hook-nosed gentleman dressed in a slack gray suit, wrinkled beige shirt and bolo tie. He appeared to be well beyond retirement age and had a deformed leg or hip that forced him to walk with a pronounced limp (a favorite pastime on second Smith would be imitating him kicking a metaphysical trash can around the classroom), but he was vigorous and expressively energetic, and it was apparent he loved his subject.

Sloan was the only professor I had that first semester who was an author. He'd written at least two books, one of which was the class text, *A Survey of the Old Testament*. I'd purchased a used copy a few days earlier, and I'd read the first chapter during a quiet afternoon when I'd opted out of one of the religious gatherings that dominated freshman orientation.

Sloan's writing was easily comprehended—there were no words of more than three syllables unless they were biblical placenames—and his subject matter was presented in a straightforward manner. Moreover, the ambitious student who'd previously owned my copy of the text had underlined all the pertinent passages so that it was possible to skim the chapters and focus on only those sections that were the highlights of Sloan's lectures, each of which would be the basis for a quiz given at the beginning of the next class. It was all so simple—and convenient. If I skipped a class session or my attention waned during one of Sloan's lectures, I could read the chapter, memorize the highlighted passages, and pass the quiz with no problem. Sloan made it clear at the outset that he wasn't teaching a course in the spiritual mysteries of religion but rather a contemporary explanation of the Old Testament. What caused the plague of locusts? What is the nature of hell? This suited me fine. I didn't believe in the Old Testament. Or the New.

I was out of class by noon and standing in line at McEwen. I ate lunch with Gene, Tindall, Maynard, and my sullen roommate, who had dragged himself out of bed, looking not much improved for having slept all morning. We offered insights about our professors and their purported eccentricities picked up from upperclassmen: "Elder is the hardest teacher on campus." "Latham's quizzes are on file in a fraternity house." "For God's sake don't take Betty Gerow's English course; she's the toughest member of the English Department." And of course: "Tully Reed is the Loch Ness Monster."

That's when I made my announcement: "I've got Reed for Freshman Comp."

A silence fell over our little gathering.

"Are you going to drop the course?" Gene asked.

I couldn't drop Reed's course. I needed those three credit hours to maintain my full-time status to secure my 2-S draft designation. I'd rather fail Reed's course than get drafted and suffer through basic training and end up in Asia. It was simply a matter of self-preservation. More importantly, I had this notion that I might be able to write something worth reading, and I was willing to take the outside chance that I'd learn a thing or two in Reed's class. At the very least, I intended to hang on until the drop-add period ended.

"No," I said valiantly. "I'm going to stick it out. I'm not afraid of Reed."

I was lying, of course. I was half scared to death of the man.

By the time we'd finished lunch, the sky had cleared, and the five of us stepped out into warm sunshine. In the green space in front of West dorm, three cutesy freshman girls were struggling at launching a kite but were having no luck catching a breeze. They flitted back and forth across the soggy lawn, the kite twisting up and down behind them. Maynard stopped and yelled, "Hey, we need more tail!" The girls allowed the kite to settle on the grass, put their hands on their hips in mock peevishness, and stared at Maynard. I felt a surge of pride. I was hanging out with a slick bunch of bandits.

# Five

By the first week of October, the suffocating Carolina heat and humidity had begun to abate. The temperature during the day hovered in the mid-80s, and at night it dipped into the upper 50s. I pushed up my dorm window and dozed with my father's Navy blanket pulled to my chin. Gashes in the red earth laid open for the installation of the new steam pipes were filled in and seeded with ryegrass, and the accompanying mud began to disappear. The noon sky that domed the walled campus was an excruciating blue, and the leaves on the oaks and poplars took on a touch of autumn color.

As with most freshmen, the opening days of classes—mid-September and into early October—were my first taste of absolute freedom, and oddly enough, I found myself a victim of my parents' nagging. At home I had to be told repeatedly to make my bed and keep my room neat. "I refuse to pay you to pick up your underwear," my father was fond of saying. Now that I was in college, I kept my room clean and my bed made, carefully tucking in the corners and stretching the blanket tight so my side of the room was presentable. Each Wednesday night, I dutifully toted my dirty sheets, pillowcase, cheap terrycloth towels, and ratty washcloths down to the first floor to exchange for clean linens.

If this change in my habits was the result of my parents' instruction, it was also a response to my roommate's precipitous decline. In the time we shared room 218, Carl never once exchanged his sheets for clean ones, and the pile of dirty laundry on his desk had spilled onto the floor beside his bed and included many of the garments he'd so neatly arranged in the closet on the first day of orientation. He'd sold off most of his bottles of cologne for beer money, and, as nearly as I could determine, he'd quit going to class altogether.

Most of the guys on second Smith, myself included, rolled out of bed early in the morning, shuffled off to lectures, studied as little as possible, and drank beer and ate pickled eggs at the Tap Room on Friday and Saturday nights. What else was there to do? Carl disappeared every afternoon, and I grew irritated when he came stumbling in at 1 or 2 in the morning. And I began to recognize in myself a trait that was a whole lot less endearing than obsessive bed-making. I was needling Carl, heaping upon him a combination of sarcasm and spitefulness, a trait I'd no doubt inherited from my father.

"Looking good this morning," I'd say. "Let's see, that's—what?—the fourth time you've worn that shirt this week?" or "Why don't you sleep at the Tap Room? Save yourself the trouble of hitching back here and waking me up."

My scorn was doing nothing to improve Carl's self-image—and I knew it. I was consciously egging him on. I'd inherited Grandmother Drager's contempt for alcoholics, and I recalled her oft-repeated maxim: "A good man gone wrong is a bad man found out." Maybe I wanted to see Carl flunk out, so I wouldn't have to feign geniality. Maybe I wanted the room all to myself.

In my defense, I wasn't the only one ragging on Carl. He'd

become the target of ridicule up and down the hall. Tindall was on his case, and even good-natured Witt Halle occasionally landed a sarcastic sucker punch. Only Gene Matthews, who wasn't mean-natured, and Steve Maynard, who kept his own counsel, overlooked Carl's foibles. By the beginning of October, I'd resolved to move out of 218 and find a new roommate on second Smith.

The only available bed was in 202 at the Haggard Avenue end of the hall. Jim Brinkley, a sophomore dorm proctor, occupied the room, and I knocked on his door during the second week in October to ask if I could bunk with him.

"Do you fart a lot?" he asked.

I swore I didn't, and he said, "Move your stuff in."

On an afternoon when Carl was knocking back brews at the Tap Room, I gathered my belongings, toted them down the hall to 202 and made myself at home. I didn't leave a note to explain my disappearance, which was a further indication of my contempt for Carl, and when I happened to run into him a day or two later, I said I'd found an empty bed in a corner room, which I claimed was larger than the standard room. "That's fine," he said. We were both beyond caring.

I liked Brinkley. He knew how things worked at Elon and was happy to give me advice on campus survival. Thin and energetic, he hung around our room in his Fruit of the Looms and cracked one joke after another, most of them mildly scatological. "Who fired that shot?" he'd ask at least once a day and then, in a display of old-world charm, he'd lift his leg and fart—but he was otherwise a convivial roommate, a definite improvement over Carl.

So life on second Smith settled into a pattern. On weekday afternoons a few of us gathered in one of our rooms to talk ourselves into a little harmless mischief. On one such occasion, Tindall and I burned our draft cards—in my case it was my classification card—for the fun of it. One afternoon, we took turns reading aloud from Hubert Selby's *Last Exit to Brooklyn*. We marveled at the pornographic passages and the disturbing violence. It was startling stuff, cruel beyond anything I'd ever read, and the merciless prose made me long for P.G. Wodehouse's convoluted lightheartedness. Tindall produced a paperback copy of the *Kama Sutra*, which we also read aloud, augmenting passages with the appropriate animal noises. Since none of us had access to a willing female partner, we soon lost interest in the book.

At the far end of the hall, Tandy Brown, a curly-headed banjo picker, and Danny Moore, who had hoped to play football but didn't make the team, hosted an ongoing blackjack game. Unfortunately, I didn't have enough cash to be a serious player, and I lacked the skill and patience to sit through more than three hands. But I learned not to hit seventeen when playing against the dealer, a lesson that would stand me in good stead. Tindall also owned a well-worn copy of *Hoyle's Rules of Games* and we tried unsuccessfully to learn a variety of card games, including a form of Swedish whist that inevitably made my head hurt.

• • •

"Can you get me a date?" I asked Townie one morning before class.

Townie was our occasional chauffeur to the Tap Room, and I occupied the desk next to his in Stokes' history course. He was a local guy and very much a Southerner in dress, with his tasseled loafers, bowl-cut blond hair and laidback demeanor. We'd been friendly since the beginning of the semester and now, three weeks into classes, we'd become fast friends. He'd told me his given first name, which was Jim or Bob or Al, but I kept forgetting, calling him Bill or Joe or whatever popped into my head. Finally, I suggested, "Why don't I call you Townie?" Nicknames were a popular means of redefining each new friend and "Townie" seemed to suit him. He appeared to like it, smiling whenever I employed this slightly pejorative appellation.

"A date. You mean like a blind date?"

"Yeah, a blind date with a high school girl who might have a car and who likes to dance."

I was confident my $25 for the month had been deposited into my checking account, and I could maybe afford a cheap night on the town with a local girl.

"Sure," he said. "When do you want to go?"

"This Saturday would be fine with me. Can we double date? I don't have a car."

"Yeah. Saturday is good with me. We can play miniature golf or go to a movie or something."

After dinner on the Friday evening before my first college date, Tindall and I hitched into downtown Burlington and patronized the B&B Smoke Shop across from the State Theatre. We ordered a couple of drafts from a balding middle-aged bartender who had a tumor the size of a ripe plum protruding from the left side of his neck. I'd relayed to Tindall the details of the date Townie was lining up, but he was skeptical. "Man, you don't know what you'll end up with. She might be a dog. Did you ask him for a picture?"

"That wouldn't have been polite," I said. "I mean, the guy is fixing me up with a friend of his girlfriend's. How bad could she be?"

Tindall laughed. "Pretty damn bad."

"I gotta start somewhere," I said, "and it's better than hanging out at the Tap Room every Friday and Saturday night."

When the bartender asked if we wanted another beer, Tindall said, "My friend here has a date with a local girl tomorrow night.

Got any advice for him?"

"I've got what he needs right here," the bartender said, and from beneath the bar he produced a bottle of De-Lāy pills, which were supposed to prevent, according to the minimalist labeling, "the shame of premature ejaculation," making it possible for an excitable freshman such as myself to perform sexually for hours on end. "You'll be needing this stuff," the bartender assured me—like I'd be satisfying hordes of sexually demanding girls in the near future. Or ever. I was tempted to shell out $2, but only because the bottle of De-Lāy struck me as an interesting novelty item. I could imagine the laughs I'd get back in the dorm—"Got a hot date? Try some of my De-Lāy. It's only $2 a pill"—but I couldn't be wasting money on such foolishness.

More within my price range were the twenty-five-cent condoms dispensed by the four grimy vending machines that lined the wall in the men's room. Scratched and faded decals of women with '40s pompadours or cascading waves of loose-hanging hair covered each machine. These lucky models appeared to be in various stages of sexual rapture, produced no doubt by the condoms the machine would dispense. One machine advertised condoms "ribbed for her pleasure" for the unselfish male whose only thought was the gratification of his partner. Others sported a "reservoir tip." The condoms were sold for the "prevention of disease only," labeling that belied the facial expressions of the women pictured on the machines. I eeny-meeny-miny-moed and cranked a quarter into one of the apparatuses. Out dropped a square cellophane packet that I inserted into a compartment of my Madras wallet, where it would remain well beyond its expiration date, inconspicuous as a tractor tire under a rug.

On the appointed evening, Townie and his girlfriend picked me up in the parking lot of Smith dorm at 7 p.m. It was a clear night, the cool air soft and bracing, and I'd gone to some lengths to dress appropriately in a clean paisley shirt and khaki slacks, both of which I'd had laundered at the dry cleaners on Williamson Avenue, where I cashed a check for $12 to cover the night's expenses.

"What's this girl's name?" I asked, as I climbed into the back seat of Townie's blue two-door, fender-skirted '61 Chevy.

"Sarah Jean," he said. "She's real nice and a lot of fun."

We drove east on Haggard to Webb Avenue, past the car lots, barbecue restaurants and Glen Raven Mills, as a 45 rpm RCA record player mounted under the dash banged out "Thank You John" ad nauseum. I had thought it impossible to have a working record player in a car, but the machine functioned reasonably well, except when we hit a bump or rolled over railroad tracks, which was often enough on Webb Avenue to send the needle skipping and skidding along the record's surface until Townie reached down and banged the record player with the heel of his hand.

We pulled up in front of a paint-bare, one-story millhouse that stood anonymously in a line of similarly dilapidated dwellings off an avenue that emptied onto Fisher Street. I was momentarily taken aback by the condition of the home. Sections of drop siding had fallen away and the front entrance was only a step or two removed from the traffic roaring up and down the narrow street. A roof gutter had collapsed into a tangle of dead shrubbery that had grown haphazardly over the windows. But I wasn't discouraged. Beautiful women could live in ramshackle houses like in the Four Seasons' "Rag Doll" or Billy Joe Royal's "Down in the Boondocks," which is exactly where we were, albeit urban boondocks.

I hurried onto the front stoop and knocked on the wooden screened door, the stiles rattling against the frame. The windowless interior door opened on a cadaverous stringy-haired, graying woman in a blue apron and faded flowered dress. She was smoking a cigarette, her free hand on her hip, and her shoulders slumped forward.

"Is Sarah Jean here?" I asked.

"Yeah, she's here," she said, gruffly. "You might as well come on in." She gave me the once over, her eyes dark with a deeply ingrained antagonism, and pushed open the screen door. The tiny living room was as bleak as the exterior of the house. Furnished with a threadbare patternless rug, two shabby easy chairs, a ladder-back rocker with a Victorian pattern pressed into the cresting rail, and a cheap floor lamp. The room reeked of cigarettes. The mottled walls were stained nicotine brown, and a black-and-white TV flickered against a wall covered with ancient sepia photographs of emaciated, bearded men and angry, overweight women frowning, bent and distracted, silhouetted in front of shotgun houses and tobacco barns.

Below the photographs, a man in dark green work pants and a tight white T-shirt was kicked back in one of the easy chairs reading the *Times-News*, a lit cigarette dangling loosely between his fingers. He didn't look up as I stepped into the room but shook out the newspaper and deliberately held it in front of his face.

"Sarah Jean, there's a boy here who says he wants to see ya," the woman called out in a weary, petulant voice.

Standing in that living room at dusk on that October evening, I realized that I wasn't in Annapolis anymore. I'd been observing Burlington's neighborhoods as my buddies and I hitched to the Tap Room and back, and I'd come to realize there wasn't an abundance of middle-class homes. A gated country club, no doubt home to mill owners and executives, was located a few blocks from the Tap Room, and I observed an occasional brick, ranch-style house as we zigzagged from Elon to Church Street, but most of the dwellings in the downtown were tiny, wood-framed one-story structures that probably dated from the turn of the century. These "millhouses" were scattered in groups of three or four in areas zoned for commercial use, tiny dwellings situated among gas stations, used car lots, and convenience stores, and it occurred to me that the Great Depression, even in the fall of 1965, had not quite let loose of the South. Judging from the number of mills, a sizable percentage of the population worked in the cotton industry, servicing spinning and weaving machines or whatever else went on in those stark brick buildings. I'd heard a few of my dorm friends—Southerners only—describe these folks as "lint heads," a pejorative term that referred to any worker who eked out a living in the mill culture and any of their kin, regardless of how they earned their keep. Now I'd come face-to-face with these people and they seemed to regard me as the enemy, even though I was, at heart, sympathetic to their plight. I was a member of the social class that had discarded them, a pampered son of the upwardly mobile. My family wasn't rich—we were only one generation removed from these mill workers, and we survived from paycheck to paycheck—but I'd grown up in a '50s split-level, and my parents purchased, on the installment plan, a new car every couple of years. These were the people who carded the cotton, doffed the bobbins, and wove the cloth for the clothing I was wearing. And as far as they were concerned, I might as well have been from Mars. Even though Maryland was south of the Mason-Dixon Line, they'd heard my accent and they probably considered me a Yankee, a creature to be, at the very least, mistrusted.

 A russet-haired, gaunt girl garbed in a washed-out, wrinkled blue dress stepped from behind a blue curtain that separated the living room and kitchen. She wasn't unattractive, but her face appeared locked in a permanent frown and her eyes were red and puffy as if she'd been crying. The shopworn, mill-town background flamed out at me. Her dress may have been made from the same material as the curtain, which was only slightly less faded, and she was wearing scuffed white go-go boots. I introduced myself, and she stared at me quizzically. "Make sure you're back here early," the graying woman said curtly. "No later than 10, and I mean it."

"I'll have her back on time," I promised, playing the obliging gentleman and already wishing that my first blind date might somehow end instantly.

"Yeah," the woman said, rubbing out her cigarette in an ashtray wobbling on the threadbare arm of the unoccupied easy chair. "Make sure you do." My date and I walked silently to the blue Chevy and slid into the back seat.

"We can play miniature golf," Townie suggested.

"That's fine," I replied. And we drove a mile to a course on Church Street.

I paid for the first round and made polite conversation, but Sarah Jean remained silent, tapping her golf ball so tentatively that it took us a good thirty minutes to get around the course once. I tried to initiate a conversation by asking what subjects she was studying in high school, to which she responded, "Regular stuff." When I asked what she planned to do after graduation, she looked away and didn't answer, so I let it drop.

With nothing better to do, I suggested we play a second round, which we did in complete silence, tapping the balls between the blades of a rotating miniature Dutch windmill, through a plaster-of-Paris castle, and over a water hazard. Once or twice I tried to encourage Sarah Jean—"Nice shot" or "Good one"—but she didn't respond. And I began to wonder if I'd done or said something offensive. She hadn't smiled. Not once.

Sarah Jean offered her only spontaneous pronouncement of the evening at 8:15: "Take me home," she said. And by 8:30 I was again standing on her front stoop, holding open the rickety screen door, traffic whooshing by two feet from my backside. "Thank you," I said, although I couldn't imagine what I was thanking her for. She turned and disappeared into the smoky living room, the front door slamming shut behind her.

Townie dropped me in the parking lot of Smith dorm so he and his date could enjoy the remainder of the evening. "Man, I'm sorry about Sarah Jean," he said, as I stepped out onto the asphalt. "Usually she's lots of fun. I don't know what was wrong with her tonight."

"I appreciate your getting me a date," I said, handing him a buck to cover my share of the gas.

"Not a problem," he said, and dropped the Chevy in gear and rumbled off, Willie Tee still warbling on his record player.

Back on second Smith, I mentioned my date with Sarah Jean to Tindall. He laughed. "I warned you."

Gene Matthews was no more sympathetic. "Well, that's strike two," he said.

I did the best I could to put the evening out of my mind. But the disastrous blind date continued to haunt me. What had I done to make Sarah Jean and her parents dislike me so? Had I dressed inappropriately? Maybe they flat-out didn't like my looks. I sure as hell wasn't a Shag Boy, although I doubted Sarah Jean ran with that clique. She didn't have the loot to buy the accouterments. Nice girls didn't dance the Shag in white go-go boots. Mostly I wondered if I'd suffer similar rejections from all the Southern girls I was likely to meet. For all my careful preparation, my social life was anything but promising.

I ran into Townie the next week in McEwen Dining Hall. "I got some news for you," he said. "Your date the other night had just told her parents she was pregnant."

"What the hell?" I asked in amazement.

"Yeah, some guy got her preggers, and she'd broken the happy news to her mom and dad a few hours before we picked her up."

I could imagine Sarah Jean sitting at the rickety kitchen table with her mother and father, the three of them chowing down on cornbread, barbeque, and collard greens. Then Sarah Jean begins to weep. "What the hell's wrong with you, girl?" her father asks, and she blurts out, "I'm pregnant!" God knows what transpires after that, but whatever her parents' reaction, they know Sarah Jean is going to have a baby; she has no choice. It's the law. Her childhood is over, her life altered irrevocably. She probably won't finish high school, and her parents will have another mouth to feed. Or she'll have to marry the hapless father, who is probably a high school student himself. A couple of hours later, I come knocking at the door, this chatty college kid from Yankeeland, all decked out in his preppy best and ready for a night on the town.

"Jeez," I said to Townie. "No wonder she didn't have much to say."

He laughed. "Looks to me like you made a clean getaway."

# Six

"The roman empire [sic] collapses due to economic decline, attack by barbarian tribes, and the weakening of the political and societal institutions...."

As Dr. Stokes lectured on the fall of Rome, I sat at my desk on the second floor of the Alamance Building jotting notes and watching two girls lounging on the south lawn near the mysterious O'Kelly monument. The October sky was a cloudless blue, the grass a waning gray-green, the temperature in the mid-70s: a day that invited indolence. I surmised the girls were juniors or seniors by the easy assurance with which they'd sprawled themselves on the lawn, their purses and books flung haphazardly. Their faces were blurred by the wavy green window glass and by distance—I must have been three hundred feet away—but I suspected, or imagined, they were beautiful in the way that all young mammals are beautiful: their skin supple, hair lustrous, eyes pure and bright. Both women wore print dresses, one blue and the other a brownish orange. The girl in the blue dress sat with her knees tight to her breasts, and her friend was stretched out on the grass, her chin resting on her hand, supported by her elbow. It occurred to me that human history, from a male point of view at least, resided in the downward curve from her breasts to the gentle camber of her buttocks. I have no talent as an artist, but I ceased taking notes—what did the Franks and the Visigoths have to do with my life?—and instead sketched the girls in my notebook, fitfully scribbling four crude likenesses, none of them satisfying.

As I finished my final sketch, the girls began to laugh, tossing back their heads and gesticulating excitedly with their hands, pantomiming, I suspected, an amusing encounter with a third party. My immediate thought was that some hapless freshman boy was the object of their ridicule. Perhaps he'd had the audacity to ask one of them out. "Can you imagine," the girl in blue might be saying, "this sorry little twerp walked right up to me in the cafeteria and asked me for a date? What's he got in mind, a walk down the railroad tracks and a Coke in the snack bar? How nice!"

The good news was that they weren't laughing at me. Except for my brief encounter with a potential dance partner at the orientation "social hour," I hadn't had the courage to even speak to a girl, even a freshman girl, who lived on campus. In the five weeks I'd spent in North Carolina only thirteen meaningful words had been spoken to me by women: "I don't know how to dance like that" and "I want to go home," leaving me with a crippling sense of inadequacy.

North Carolina Woman's College in Greensboro, the home to thousands of wanton females, might as well have been in China. I had no car, no money, and no chance of getting a date—and I wouldn't have a social life until I managed to somehow get my hands on enough cash to borrow a car and pay for a night on the town. Even then, I had to find a woman willing to go out with a geek who couldn't dance correctly.

I was considering this when Dr. Stokes spoke my name aloud at the conclusion of his lecture. "Mr. Smith," he said, yanking me back into reality, "would you see me in my office at 2 o'clock?" Startled, I looked up and wondered, as I usually did at such moments, who and where I was. I'd been working hard at maintaining my anonymity, and now the professor had singled me out in front of the class.

"Yes, sir," I managed to gasp and then fled the room with the other students. I was due in Poli-Sci in ten minutes.

I skipped lunch and hurried back to the dorm to grapple with my overactive imagination, settling on a likely scenario: I'd knock at Dr. Stokes' office door, and he'd invite me inside and direct me to the wooden school chair I'd occupied when we'd worked out my fall schedule a few weeks before. "Now, Mr. Smith," he'd say. "I couldn't help but notice that during today's lecture you weren't paying attention. You had the look of someone whose mind was somewhere else. Is something bothering you?"

I'd have to tell the truth: "No, I wasn't thinking about anything."

"Well," Dr. Stokes would say, displeasure evident in his pained expression, "if you can't pay careful attention during my lectures, I'll have to ask that you . . ."

I'd have to drop his class, or maybe I'd get lucky and only receive a stern reprimand. I needed Western Civ to maintain my full-time status.

I considered marching into Dr. Stokes' office and boldly offering an implausible excuse. "I want to apologize," I'd blurt out before he could utter a word. "My entire family was killed in an airplane crash last week, and I've had trouble concentrating ever since." Or maybe a more pitiable and less verifiable contrivance would suffice: "I was recently diagnosed with an inoperable brain tumor, and I only have a few months to live, so naturally my concentration has tended to . . ."—which would necessitate my dying once the semester was over.

By 1:45 p.m., I could stand the suspense no longer and clambered down the stairs and out the side door of Smith. Dr. Stokes' office was in a temporary white clapboard building next to Mooney. Inside the front entrance there was a bulletin board on which someone had thumbtacked a piece of paper on which was written in Magic Marker:

> God is Dead.
> Nietzsche
> Nietzsche is Dead.
> God

Who the hell was Nietzsche? I paused to ponder the meaning of the notice, and then, utterly nonplussed, hurried along, the plywood floor flexing with each step, and knocked lightly at Dr. Stokes' door. "Come in," I heard him say. I turned the knob and stepped tentatively into the sparsely furnished office. Dr. Stokes directed me with a wave of his hand to sit in my regular chair directly in front of his cluttered desk. So far my imagination was right on the money.

"Occasionally we make sacrifices that will contribute to the college experience," Dr. Stokes began, his deeply etched face deadly serious, "and such a situation presents itself now. I know you have a lot of studying to do, but I'm hoping you'll take an hour or so to contribute to the betterment of your education and that of your fellow students."

"Yes, sir," I said, hardly believing my luck.

"Tomorrow evening we are having a distinguished speaker, Dr. Francis Butler Simkins, at the Liberal Arts Forum. He's a well-known Southern scholar, and he's going to lecture on the South and how it's changed in recent times. I need someone to set up forty folding chairs in the lobby of West dormitory, and I thought you might help out."

"Yes, sir," I said again, a warm surge of relief coursing through my body. "I'll be glad to."

"Tomorrow afternoon at 3 p.m., go to West dorm, and you'll find the chairs stacked in the lobby. You should arrange them in a semicircle facing the lectern, leaving plenty of room for folks to stretch their legs. Make sure everything is neatly arranged." He paused. "Can you do that?"

"I can do it," I said, and I was out of there.

I was flattered Dr. Stokes had thought of me, even if the task was menial. He must have considered me reliable, and that had to be good. I figured, too, that I might get the benefit of the doubt when it came time to hand out the grades. I had a B average in Dr. Stokes' class. Perhaps setting up a few chairs would land me an A. It couldn't hurt.

On Tuesday afternoon, I hoofed it over to the lobby of West dorm and made a great show of unfolding the metal chairs and arranging them in front of the lectern. It took fifteen minutes of clanking and banging and another twenty minutes of positioning the chairs to leave appropriate legroom and create space so the audience could move up and down the aisles. Whenever a girl entered or exited the lobby, I made a point of manhandling the chairs with an enviable flourish.

Stepping back to scan my handiwork, I was pleased. The room retained its formal air despite the gray metal chairs. In a few hours, Dr. Stokes would step to the podium. I imagined him addressing the crowd: "Before we begin this evening's lecture," he'd say in a solemn voice, "I want to thank Mr. Smith for taking the time to arrange the chairs for tonight's lecture. He's done a beautiful job. If all students were as helpful as Mr. Smith, this would be a better world." And the room would erupt in applause. I'd stand and smile, bowing slightly from the waist.

That evening, I shrugged on my Harris Tweed sports jacket, twisted a Windsor knot in a red-striped tie, and marched over to the dorm in the cool October air, my notebook and pen at the ready in case Dr. Stokes asked me to reprise the lecture in the next Western Civ class. The lounge was full of the bustle and rhythm particular to such academic occasions, and the dim light from the shaded 60-watt table lamps provided an intimate glow. The chairs I'd arranged were taken, and I sat with Tindall and fifteen other rumpled freshman boys on the floor near the front entrance. Dr. Stokes stepped up to the microphone, his brow furrowed and his bright eyes surveying the room. A respectful hush fell over the audience as he offered his simple and direct introduction, listing Dr. Simkins' books, *A History of the South* and *The Everlasting South* in particular, and detailing his other academic achievements. Unfortunately, he neglected to mention my name, which was a trifle disturbing. Being a toady has few rewards.

Simkins, a jowly, balding, bespectacled man with a mousey gray mustache, was a Southern progressive, a liberal in the context of the time. He was an adamant supporter of the Civil Rights Movement, although I gathered that his notions concerning race in the South were more complex than he had time to express. Simkins viewed the contemporary white Southerner as incapable of changing his attitude toward his black brethren. "We cannot transform the hearts and minds of those who've been reared to reject change," he said, "and perhaps that's just as well. In accepting integration, we must preserve what's good in the old South." Or that's what I wrote in my notebook.

Race was the dominant issue of the time, more so than the war in Vietnam. But as Simkins spoke, I realized the simple truth:

I didn't know any black people. When I was a child in the '50s living in Easton, Maryland, my mother had a part-time job as a telephone operator, and she hired a succession of black women—Evelyn, Algae, and Cecilia are names I recall—who came to our house to do the ironing and cleaning. Although I was friendly with these women, they were little more than acquaintances. The integration of my elementary school occasioned the obligatory white backlash, but my father, ever the contrarian, led me through a white picket line so I could take my seat in a classroom at Hanson Street Elementary School. While I was attending high school in Annapolis, there was only one black student in the class of '65, Michael Strong, a pleasant, diminutive kid who had a locker next to mine in gym class. But I couldn't claim to have ever had a conversation with him. In my four weeks at Elon, I'd seen only one black student on campus, and he must have been a commuter student. But if my knowledge of the black community was sorely lacking, I was full of pseudo-fervor for the movement and viewed myself as a liberal on race relations. I was convinced that black people in America had been mistreated—an insight that didn't require exceptional powers of observation—and their rights needed to be guaranteed. I made a point of never using racial epithets, although many of my new Southern friends weren't so inclined.

The lecture was followed by the obligatory Q and A session during which a student asked Dr. Simkins if he thought white Southerners would ever abandon their racial prejudices. The good doctor stared straight ahead, his face expressionless. "The question of race in the South will never be resolved until whites and Negros have intermarried in large enough numbers to blur racial distinctions," he said, "and I don't see that happening in our lifetime."

Sitting next to Tindall was a freshman from Connecticut whose hand shot instantly into the air. I hadn't met this student, but Tindall was friendly with him and had nicknamed him, in a teasing way, Liberal Swine. He was a thin, angular guy who bore a sickly resemblance to Mick Jagger. His thick brown hair hung down over his collar and wavy bangs drooped onto his broad forehead. "I'm from Connecticut," the student said, standing tall among those of us seated on the floor. "I have a black girlfriend at home, and we intend to get married when I graduate."

A palpable intaking of breath punctuated the subsequent silence. "Well," Simkins replied, "that would be a beginning." And the program abruptly ended. I stayed to help the janitor fold and put away the chairs, then strolled back to my room and crawled into bed.

Later that night, I awakened to a disturbance in the hall—cursing, yelling, maybe even a muted scream—but commotions of all sorts were so common in the dorm that I took little notice. I flipped over my pillow and dozed off. It wasn't until the following morning that I heard a rumor that a group of football players had hunted down the kid from Connecticut and roughed him up. As terrible as this sounded, I was skeptical. I hadn't seen any football players at Simkins' lecture. They weren't known for frequenting programs sponsored by the Liberal Arts Forum. So, I dismissed the entire episode as nothing more than adolescent blather.

Dr. Stokes used the class period following Simkins' lecture to discuss the 1870 lynching of Wyatt Outlaw, a former slave and Union soldier, at the courthouse in Graham. "They left him hanging from a tree in front of the courthouse and no one would remove the body because they didn't want to incur the wrath of the Klan," Dr. Stokes explained. The sad story of Wyatt Outlaw struck me as distant and irrelevant, but I listened intently and took notes on what Dr. Stokes referred to as the Kirk-Holden War, which, like everything else in America, had to do with race.

By the end of the month, Liberal Swine had disappeared. He'd packed up his gear and headed home to Connecticut. There was no explanation as to why he'd gone, but I connected his abrupt disappearance with the disturbance I'd heard on the hall following the Simkins lecture.

A few days later, Tindall burst into my room. "Come with me," he said. "You gotta see this." I followed him to the nearest bathroom, where he yanked open a stall and pointed to an epistle scrawled in blue Magic Marker on the inside of the door. The lengthy message was from Liberal Swine, and although I didn't memorize what he'd written, I recall that he was taking the South to task for its racism, and that he was bidding us a bitter farewell.

His parting comments made no difference whatsoever, and none of the other freshmen on second Smith ever spoke of the Connecticut kid again. His shocking admission about dating a black woman was instantly forgotten. If his alleged encounter with angry students, football players or otherwise, was reported to the administration, I never heard, although at a gathering a few weeks later the dean warned us not to write research papers that required us to contact the Ku Klux Klan, which was no doubt good advice.

I wasn't the least troubled by Liberal Swine's departure. I convinced myself that this alleged harassment of a fellow student was nothing more than a joke, that those who threatened and abused him were making light of the situation, acting out a silly parody of their elders' more sinister rituals. The sit-ins at the Greensboro Woolworth's, twenty miles to the west of Elon, were five years gone. The world had changed for the better. Racism was a thing of the past.

In our daily lives, we were acknowledging the absurdity of the human condition. I understood that laughter was the only appropriate response to irrationality—after all, God had killed

Nietzsche—and that the attitudes of our fathers' generation were too radically oppressive to be compared to those of our own more enlightened time. So why not poke fun? Racial injustice was a regrettable but persistent social nuisance that had its heyday in the distant past.

    I was wrong.

# Seven

October 15, 1965

Dear Mom and Dad,

I'm writing because I need some extra money to have my loafers repaired. I was walking back from class yesterday when I tore a seam on my left loafer, and when I examined the shoe in my room, I could see that it couldn't be stitched back together. The leather had torn and pulled away from the shoe like in this drawing:

It makes it hard to walk in the shoe, and I'm afraid that it will fall apart if I'm caught in the rain.

What I need is a new pair of loafers—the shoes are a year old and down at the heels—but I can't afford to buy such a high-priced item with the money you've been sending me. I'm already broke and it's only the 15th. To get through to the end of the month I need $50 so that I can buy school supplies and food and incidentals like typing paper, deodorant, a new typewriter ribbon, and other stuff, including a new pair of shoes.

Otherwise, things are going well here. I'm making pretty good grades.

Your Son,
Stephen

PS—I've moved out of the room with Carl and I'm in 202 Smith with Jim Brinkley. He's a junior and a real good guy.

My left shoe did have a tear in the leather, although it was not nearly as extreme as I depicted in my drawing and the shoe wasn't about to disintegrate. What I needed, of course, was cash. The measly $25 my parents deposited in my checking account at the beginning of October had slipped through my fingers like water, or, depending on how truthful I was inclined to be, like beer. If I tossed in a few chili and slaw hot dogs from Zack's, incidental sodas

I cranked from the drink machine on second Smith, the quarters I dropped into coin-operated washing machines, a two-dollar haircut, and three bucks a month at the laundry where I was having my shirts starched and pressed—a compulsory extravagance if I wanted to keep up appearances—my financial circumstance was dismal.

Unlike my former roommate, who had taken up full-time residency at the Tap Room, I hadn't fallen into the proverbial bottle, but I was enjoying a frosty beverage with friends a couple of times a week and at least once on the weekend. I wasn't getting drunk or even tipsy, but I was putting away two or three mugs during each visit. And I'd developed an addiction to pickled eggs. I didn't have any bottles of cologne to sell, or any possessions anyone wanted to buy. And I wasn't going to borrow money from my friends. I had too much pride for that. After all, Carl was into everyone on the hall for a couple of bucks, and after ridiculing him in public, I couldn't turn around and do what he was doing. That would have been flat-out mortifying.

When I posted my letter on the 15th, I had $3.50 to last me for the remainder of the month. If my parents took pity on me and deposited another $25 in my account, I could get my shoe repaired for $3—I'd already gotten an estimate from a cobbler in Burlington—and I'd have the remainder of the cash to squander on sundries.

I read the letter carefully and decided it was well-reasoned and written in businesslike prose with the right touch of pathos. The cincher was my deceptive drawing, which illustrated the supposedly sad condition of the shoe, but after I dropped the letter in the outgoing mail, it occurred to me that I'd erred in asking for $25 more a month, a greedy one hundred percent increase. My sad epistle would only anger my parents, and they wouldn't be inclined to cough up another cent. I should have requested only $10, a more reasonable sum.

I was right. Five days after I'd posted my appeal for more cash, I peered into my mailbox and spied an envelope resting slantways against the glass. I hurriedly removed it and recognized my father's semi-cursive scrawl. I knew it was bad news:

October 19, 1965

Stephen,

Your mother and I are sorry to hear about your shoe, but you're going to have to take care of it yourself. The money we deposit in your account each month is all we can afford, and you need to learn to budget your expenditures accordingly. Take your grandmother's advice and wear your tennis shoes.

That would have been enough of an answer, but the old man then launched into an extended metaphor that ran for five handwritten pages. He compared my life at college to a ship sailing the "high seas." I was the captain of the ship, and he was down in the engine room shoveling coal into the boiler. He had no idea where the ship might sail—"I'm simply doing my job to the best of my ability," he wrote—but he noted that we'd eventually reach a critical point in our journey when the ship might continue on "proud and tall" or it might run onto the "rocks of life," destroying the ship and ruining the journey for everyone aboard, including the crew, of which he was a member, "along with anyone whose expectations depended on the skill of the captain. There are rocky shores all around you, and if the ship founders, it's the captain's fault. He'll have no one to blame but himself."

I folded the letter, returned it to its envelope, and stowed it in the drawer of my desk. Rocky shores all around me, huh? How the hell was I going to continue my weekend trips to the Tap Room if I had no money? Going on a date—if I ever managed to find a willing woman—was beyond hope.

The next evening, I placed a collect call to our house in Annapolis. My parents were usually at home after dinner, and I thought a direct appeal for a lesser amount of money might yield results. Mike answered the phone and didn't hesitate to accept the charges.

"Hey," I said, "are Mom and Dad there?"

"I don't know where they are," he answered. "I'm the only one home. They went to the store or something."

"Damn," I said.

"Out of money, aren't you?"

"Yeah, how'd you know?"

"They were talking about you at dinner the other night. They decided not to send you any more money. They think you're wasting it on beer."

"Damn," I said again.

"Dad says you're going to flunk out anyway."

"I'm not flunking out," I snapped. "My grades are pretty good. Tell him I'm doing ok."

"You'll have to tell him yourself. You know how he is; I'm staying out of his way."

"When they come in, tell them that I need more money to get my shoe fixed. It's pretty bad when you haven't got decent shoes to wear. I need some cash."

"Well, you could come back here and work at the Safeway and put up with Dad and Mom."

I gave Mike's proposal consideration, imagining what my life might be like if I returned home in defeat. It was too painful to contemplate. "Yeah, I get ya," I said. "Don't tell them I called. They'll get pissed off."

"They're pissed off most of the time anyway."

Then I got an idea: "Could you loan me five or ten bucks until Thanksgiving?"

There was silence on the other end of the line.

"Put it in an envelope and mail it to me," I suggested. "I'll pay you back when I come home."

"I don't have any money."

I knew he was lying. He usually had a few dollars stashed away. "I'll give you my Donovan record."

"I've been playing it ever since you left," he said. "Why would I pay you for it?" And he hung up in my ear.

If I did nothing but sit in the dorm for the next week and a half, my account would be flush again, but it was sad to imagine myself alone while my friends were knocking back frosty beverages and yucking it up at the Tap Room. Making it through the next few days didn't solve the long-term problem. Still, there was little I could do but bide my time.

The solution came to me in a burst of illumination: I could hitchhike home and appeal to my parents in person. If I reasoned with them face-to-face, they might give me $10 more a month, even the $25 I'd asked for. At any rate, they'd have to buy me a bus ticket back to Burlington—they'd warned me about hitchhiking—and I assumed they'd bless me with a few dollars to cover my in-transit expenses. Why not give it a try? I couldn't afford to go out with my friends anyway. Maybe I'd check in with a few old high school buds, play the big man on campus card.

If hitchhiking alone to Annapolis was risky, my fears were

partially dispelled when I heard Scott say he was driving to Richmond for the weekend. If I could catch a ride with him, I'd be halfway to Annapolis.

"Want some company?" I asked.

"Sure," he said.

I broke one of my remaining dollar bills into quarters and phoned my friend Billy King in Annapolis. Billy and I had knocked around in high school, and he was a good man to know if you needed transportation. He loved to drive, and he had the best cars—a 409 Chevy, the first Mustang in Annapolis, a GTO, cars that inspired rock songs—and I asked if he would be willing to meet me on Friday in Richmond and drive me back to Annapolis. "It's only a two-hour drive," I said.

He didn't hesitate. "Sure, what time and where?"

When my parents drove me South in September, I'd noticed a landmark on I-95. "A few miles south of Richmond there's a Philip Morris office building on the right. I'll be there by late afternoon, let's say at 4 p.m."

"You got it," he promised.

It never occurred to me that such a trip would take up most of Billy's day and cost him at least $10 in gas. I was so focused on wheedling a little cash out of my parents that I never considered my friend's expenditure in time and money.

I devoted the next afternoon and evening to studying so that I'd be caught up for the weekend, and after Friday morning classes, I tossed some underwear and socks into my high school gym bag, pulled on my Converse All Stars, lest my parents discover how I'd exaggerated the damage to my loafer (Grandmother Drager would have been proud), and Scott and I climbed into his car and headed north with the radio maxed out on rock stations. I had $1.50 in my pocket. At 3:30 p.m., Scott dropped me on the shoulder of I-95 in front of the Philip Morris office building.

The air was bracing with the first deep chill of autumn. As Scott pulled away, I found a likely spot where motorists could clearly see me but not so close to the highway as to place myself in immediate danger of being flattened by a semi. A high wire fence ran between the shoulder of I-95 and a service road that led to the office building behind me, and up the highway, half a mile or so stood a sculpted monolith advertising the Marlboro and Philip Morris brands. Beyond the sign, the highway to Annapolis lay wide open. I only needed to make my connection with Billy, and I was home free. I had thirty minutes to wait before my friend's ETA. Everything was going as planned.

• • •

I clung to a tiny, fraying thread of hope for the first few hours. Maybe Billy had gotten away late. Maybe his car had broken down, and he had to have it repaired. Maybe he'd gotten lost. I spent the remainder of the daylight hours staring north on the interstate, willing Billy's GTO to materialize out of the steady stream of cars hurtling southward. Every few minutes a vehicle that was surely Billy's—hope is stubborn stuff—would come into view, a speck at first, distant and partially obscured by hundreds of less fashionable cars and tractor-trailer trucks. The vehicle would gradually come into focus, emerge full throttle into my immediate vision and then whoosh by me, disappearing in a shuttering blast of carbon dioxide.

During the first four hours, three Virginia state troopers decked out in their starched gray and blue uniforms and shiny black shoes stopped to inform me that there was no hitchhiking allowed on I-95. I'd anticipated their arrival and quickly pointed out to them in my most plaintive tone that I wasn't hitchhiking. "A friend is going pick me up any minute now," I explained. Two of the troopers went about their business. "Stand over on the grassy side of the shoulder," the last trooper said. "If I come by here again and find you still waiting, I'll have to remove you from the highway. It's too dangerous to stand so close to the road. You could easily get hit by someone who's not paying attention."

As dusk gradually drifted across the surrounding countryside, the horizon streaked azure and slate gray. Traffic seemed to increase with the coming of darkness, a constant stream of cars and trucks headed God knows where, their headlights momentarily illuminating the highway south. With the onset of night, I was forced to move closer to the road so that Billy would be able to see me, thus placing myself in ever-increasing danger. I had to weigh my proximity to the steady torrent of traffic against my visibility, and I found myself moving forward and then stepping back into the shadows with the approach of traffic, the cars and trucks seeming to come at me in clusters.

To pass the time I played mind games. If I spotted a GTO—or any late model Pontiac—that was a positive sign. After all, it stood to reason that GTOs begat GTOs. Billy was no doubt headed my way, approaching with the instancy of light, and it was a question of when an anonymous Pontiac would magically transform itself into the GTO that would rescue me.

I knew how it would go. Billy's car would appear first as a tiny dot of light emerging from a focal point on the northern horizon, then it would gradually assume the appropriate shape and color until it emerged from the similitude of the traffic that surrounded it and pulled onto the shoulder, cinders popping under its hot tires. I'd climb in and we'd be headed home.

But that didn't happen. Each new Pontiac I spied shuddered by me, leaving in its wake a mild sense of desolation. I switched to Mustangs, which were more plentiful on the highway. When a

Mustang passed me, I'd look for Maryland tags, another sign that Billy would arrive with my next breath. Then I tried four-hole Buicks, Corvairs, and '57 Chevys, which were exceedingly rare. My prospects dwindled with each passing minute.

At 9 p.m., I underwent an out-of-body experience. I imagined I was driving one of the cars speeding toward me, and I could see myself, a forlorn teenager waiting for a ride on the side of the dark interstate. Why not give him a lift back to North Carolina? I asked myself with the passing of each vehicle. The answer was not encouraging: Why would I bother? I didn't know who this kid was or what he was capable of. He might be a serial killer. Why was he hitchhiking at night? He had to be in trouble; otherwise, he'd be at home with his family or friends. When it occurred to me that these strangers felt no sympathy for me, I experienced an even greater sense of loss. Why had they chosen to ignore me in my time of need? It would have been easy for any of them to pull over and ask, "Do you need a ride, friend?"

I considered putting out my thumb to catch a lift north, but that would have necessitated crossing four lanes of screaming traffic, which was too frightening to contemplate. If I survived the crossing, a state trooper might catch me hitchhiking and tote me off to jail, or wherever they took indigent teenagers.

Eventually, the darkness and the danger forced me back from the shoulder and into the crabgrass and garbage in a long, shallow drainage ditch that paralleled the containment fence. I scuffled among the beer cans, soda bottles, McDonald's wrappers, crumbled cigarette packs, and paper bags whose contents were too mysterious to inspect, and I began to make plans for the night. Billy and I weren't going to make a connection. I had $1.50 in my pocket, not enough to get a motel room, even if I could find one. I'd have to leave the highway, climb the fence and walk to a place where

I could sleep unmolested. The huge Philip Morris sign seemed a likely spot. Maybe I could take shelter there. The temperature was dropping rapidly, and I had only the outer clothing I was wearing—pants, a shirt, and a light London Fog jacket that was little more than a windbreaker. It was going to be a long, cold night.

I began to rebuke myself, realizing that my plan for getting to Annapolis was only as strong as its weakest link, which was hooking up with Billy. How could I have ever believed that I'd make it home? I was lost and alone, cold and hungry, and I had no way to phone Billy or Scott or to get in touch with anyone who might help me. By 11 p.m., I was beyond hope, and a cold, stark shudder coursed through me. I'd never felt so alone and helpless.

I was climbing the fence separating the highway from the Philip Morris building when a car came grumbling down the gravel service road, its high beams flashing on and off. It was Scott Roberson! God knows I was glad to see him. In an instant I was standing beside his car, hardly daring to believe my luck.

"What happened to your friend?" he asked, rolling down the driver's side window.

"I don't know. He must have gotten confused or lost or something."

"Climb in," he said. "You aren't going to get a ride this time of night."

In an act of kindness that outshone the generosity of all men and angels, Scott drove me to his home in Moseley, where his mother fixed me a late-night sandwich and gave me a bed to sleep in. On Saturday morning, he drove me to the Richmond bus station, bought me a ticket, and put me on the Greyhound to Annapolis, where I arrived midafternoon on Saturday. I walked the distance from West Street to Janice Drive and stomped dramatically into our living room. Mike, who was stretched out on the couch listening to his portable radio, a wire leading from the plastic box to the plug stuck in his ear, sat up when I made my unexpected entrance.

"Did you flunk out?" he asked immediately.

"No," I answered.

My mother was in the kitchen preparing dinner, rattling pots and pans. When she heard my voice, she stopped what she was doing and hurried into the living room. "What are you doing here?" she asked, her hands on her hips.

"I rode the bus home," I lied.

"I thought you were broke. Where'd you get the money?"

"I borrowed it from a friend," I explained, lying again. I couldn't tell her about my hitchhiking adventure. I realized that my trip home had been dangerous, and there was no need to worry her. Mostly, I didn't want her to know how stupid I'd been, standing on the shoulder of the interstate for seven hours, most of that time in the dark. To avoid further questions, I told her I was tired and hurried upstairs to stretch out on my bed.

At the supper table, my father, who'd been at the Academy when I arrived, also asked, "If you didn't have any money, how'd you pay for your bus ticket?"

"My friend Scott Roberson loaned me the money."

"How much do you owe him?"

"Twenty dollars." I was toting up the figures in my head. If the ticket from Richmond to Annapolis cost $8.50, then the ticket from Burlington might have cost an additional $10. The difference would be money I could put in my pocket.

"How do you propose to get back to Elon?" my mother asked.

"Guess I'll hitchhike."

My parents stared at me. "You know we don't want you hitchhiking," my father said.

"How else am I going to get back?"

"We'll pay for your bus ticket," my father griped. "But don't get in the habit of running home every couple of weeks. You should be using your time more wisely. That's why we sent you to college."

They were in no mood to discuss a raise in my allowance. Perhaps they'd be more open to such a suggestion in the morning. In the meantime, I finished supper and phoned Billy. "What the hell happened to you?" I asked.

"I don't know, man," he said. "I was there, but I didn't see you."

"I was standing on the shoulder of I-95 in front of the Philip Morris office building for seven damn hours."

"Oh, I think maybe I was on 301 and got turned around. I looked for you but figured you hadn't been able to get a lift to Richmond." He paused. "There's a party tonight. Wanna go?"

A few hours later, I was hanging out with my high school buds in a house on Porter Drive. Such parties were common in Annapolis, especially when the parents of the kid hosting the party were out of town. Most of the partygoers were high school juniors and seniors, and a few others, like myself, had graduated and were home from college for the weekend, most of them from College Park.

I expected the younger partygoers to ask me questions concerning college life—after all, I was now a college veteran and no doubt I possessed significant insights into the meaning of life—but no one was the least interested in where I'd been and what I was up to. Old girlfriends ignored me, and former buddies acted as if I'd never left Annapolis. When I gave it some thought, I realized I'd only been gone a little over five weeks, hardly time enough for anyone to notice my absence.

The next morning, my parents drove me to DC and bought me a ticket on a southbound Greyhound. Before I got on board, my father handed me $10.

"That should get you back and you'll be able to pay your friend the rest of the money you owe him when you get your allowance."

"Thanks," I said.

"We're not going to put more money in your account. You ought to be able to get by on $25 a month."

I didn't complain. I was satisfied to be headed back to North Carolina.

As we rolled south that Sunday, I watched wistfully as we blurred by the Philip Morris monolith on I-95 where I'd stood awaiting salvation two short nights before. I arrived at the bus station in Burlington a little after 10 p.m. Three Elon students, all upperclassmen, had gotten on at stops in Virginia, and we shared a cab back to the college, which cost me another buck. After the taxi dropped me at the gate in front of Smith dorm, I stood in the dark parking lot, admiring the wall that surrounded the campus. It was constructed of bricks and mortar, wasn't more than four feet high and provided no significant protection to the students living within its parameters. A lot of my new college friends thought it was silly to surround the campus with any kind of barrier—"something there is that doesn't love a wall" I remembered from high school English text—but it was comforting to know that a wall separated the college and its students, however tenuously, from a world that was indifferent and capricious.

I trudged up the stairs to the second floor, stopped by my room—Brinkley was fast asleep—and then knocked on Scott's door. "Man, thanks for taking care of me this weekend," I said. "I don't know what I would have done if you hadn't picked me up and taken me to your house. Here's some of the money I owe you, and I'll pay you the rest on the first. If there's ever anything I can do for you, all you have to do is ask." I meant what I said. The guy may well have saved my life.

Scott took the $8.50. "I'm glad I could help out," he said.

I trudged back to my room, stretched out on my bed, and reviewed the events of the weekend. I'd set out from Elon on Friday morning, and I'd stood on the shoulder of I-95 for seven interminable hours as thousands of cars streaked by me at 75 mph. It occurred to me that it would have taken only one drowsy or drunk driver to have snuffed out my life. I'd never felt as alone as I did when the sun set over Richmond on the previous Friday night. For the first time in my life, the cold ground would have been my bed. Who knows what mischief might have befallen me? Then a friend of less than two months had driven miles out of his way to save me, a sweet act of pure kindness!

Even if I didn't get a regular raise in my allowance, I'd managed to eke a few bucks out of my parents. I'd gone to a high school party where my old friends no longer seemed important to me—or I to them. All I'd wanted was to get back to Elon, safe in my dorm room. Annapolis was a world in which I no longer belonged.

• • •

During a bull session with Gene, Witt, and Tindall the following afternoon, I described my weekend hitchhiking odyssey. After two or three abortive starts, I realized that I'd begun my narrative with the most harrowing element—"So there I was standing for seven hours on the shoulder of the interstate, cars whipping by me and the sun going down and I had nowhere to go and hardly any money." Then I had to work backward and plow through the less interesting expository information—"A friend was supposed to pick me up south of Richmond but he never showed up." I was anxious to convey the feeling of euphoria I'd experienced when I walked into the dorm after a weekend spent wandering in the great void, but no one was interested. Even Tindall, who enjoyed a good yarn, was otherwise occupied. Who had time to listen to such foolishness? They hadn't stood on the shoulder of the interstate and felt an endless line of cars blast by them. My story was boring, so I calculated my gains and losses the American way—in dollars and cents. I'd left campus with $1.50, and after paying Scott the money I owed him, I had $4.50 left in my pocket. It was the hardest $3 I'd ever earned.

On the Tuesday afternoon following my adventure in hitchhiking, I knocked on the office door of the man in charge of the cafeteria. He was a thin, dark-haired business type who had lost an arm. The empty sleeve of his sports coat was pinned into the armpit of his jacket, and he was all business.

"Do you need any help in the cafeteria?"

He looked me up and down and swiveled around in his chair to remove a form from his desk drawer. "I could use you for a while each evening to help clean up the dinner dishes. It pays $1.25 an hour."

"How many hours a week?" I asked.

"Ten, maybe more. I won't need you on weekends."

I did a quick calculation in my head. It was a pittance, but it would enable me to hang out with my friends at the Tap Room. "I'll take it," I said. "When do I start?"

"Tonight."

# Eight

"It's time to write an essay," Professor Reed announced, staring at his forlorn, slack-jawed charges, a smirk on his prim face. "I doubt any of you will make a passing grade, but I'll give you an opportunity to prove yourself."

He padded catlike to the southward-facing windows and focused on a metaphysical point lost somewhere on the horizon. I craned my neck and followed his line of sight to the railroad tracks and the Victorian houses on East Trollinger Avenue, and then into the high, blue sky. The oaks had turned shades of reddish brown, the colors shimmering through the wavy green glass windowpanes.

"I'm going to allow you to choose your own topic, something with a little energy to it, a little pizzazz," he said.

I scribbled "pizzazz" in my notebook and underlined it.

"Write a narrative or an exposition or a description or whatever best suits your subject. I don't want any grammar, capitalization, punctuation, or spelling errors. You'll lose one letter grade for each mistake. Any questions?"

I wrote: "One letter grade for each mistake!!!!!" and underlined it.

"All right," he continued, "you've got until next Friday. I'll collect the essays at the end of class on that day. Now get out of here."

He didn't have to tell us twice. The six of us, survivors all, funneled out the back door and scattered like flushed quail.

I was in a panic. I had no topic. What would make Reed happy? The semester was too far gone for us to complete the four essays he'd mentioned during our first class meeting, so I might have only one opportunity to prove I was a competent writer, one chance to make a decent grade. I knew this much: Whatever I wrote had to be better than anything I'd ever written; the implications of receiving a failing grade in English 111 were far too grave to contemplate. But if I was fearful, I was also angry. Reed hadn't taught us how to write. Or, for that matter, anything else. No grammar or punctuation rules. No hints on how to choose a topic or develop an argument. He'd railed against the war, cultural intolerance, the South in general, and Lyndon Johnson in particular. The class was more sociology/political science than freshman English. Now I had to write an essay that might determine my final grade in the course, and I had no clue as to how to begin.

All I had going for me was a fanciful notion that I had a flair for writing, and it occurred to me that this glimmer of hope might well be based on self-deception. I'd made pretty good grades in high school English, and I enjoyed being creative, if it didn't involve too much thought and labor. In the tenth grade I'd written a poem titled "Footprints in the Sands of Time," a pseudo-philosophic discourse on the futility of life couched in singsongy end rhymes. The teacher, no critic of postmodern poetry, read my creation to the class, and I believed I'd done something extraordinary: I'd written a poem that the culture would not let willingly die. Mercifully, it took my peers and the teacher only thirty seconds to forget "Footprints in the Sands of Time," thus proving the poem's thesis correct.

I'd also written a short story, "A Song of Riches," in my eleventh-grade English class, and our chipmunky, toupeed teacher, Mr. Jacobson, had commented favorably on my work. Amazingly enough, my story concerned a cockfight in Baja California (I was utterly unfamiliar with both roosters and Mexico), but Jacobson claimed I was the only student who'd written a "real narrative." He read my story aloud to my thoroughly disinterested peers, who also knew nothing about roosters and Mexico.

After these two minor successes, I concluded I could write for newspapers or magazines or be a poet like the doofus in our eleventh-grade literature book who didn't have a real job and spent his time writing verse, collecting seashells and staring wistfully into Kodachrome sunsets.

So I possessed a tenuous measure of confidence: I believed I could write a good essay if I set my mind to it. But I had to come up with an appropriate topic. Since Reed had spent most of our class time—he was always late and dismissed us early—ranting about a dystopian America, I considered writing a "protest" essay. I'd attack "the establishment" and the myriad injustices the evil men in Washington were perpetrating on an unsuspecting public. I wasn't that political—not yet, anyway—I wasn't old enough to vote, and I hadn't given much thought to the war, other than how to avoid participating in it. Since I'd grown up with the navy as my family's primary source of income, I was familiar with the ways of the military, which I found generous but oppressive, and I knew that anything I had to say concerning the government was bound to be tedious and ill-informed. I considered committing to paper the story of my hitchhiking adventure, but that narrative had faltered in the telling, and I needed a dramatic tale whose contents would bring a smile to Reed's otherwise dour face.

It came to me like a flashbulb exploding in my brain: my topic would be failure. I'd heard a rumor that during the previous spring semester Reed had flunked every one of his senior English majors, and I knew from listening to his lectures, rambling as they were, that he found a perverse joy in stories of academic anguish. So and so, who'd made straight A's in high school, is admitted to college on a full academic scholarship, but at the end of the first semester "this public-school Einstein" is out on his butt, having flunked all his courses. Or "Miss High School Homecoming Queen" is unable to balance her social life with academic demands and attempts suicide by swallowing an overdose of aspirin—"She couldn't even do that right." Or "Mr. Know-It-All High School Football Captain" begins his college career as Big Man on Campus only to get booted out when he's discovered with a crib sheet secreted in his lap during his final exam in English. And so forth. Tully Reed loved a good story of comeuppance, and I was the guy who could give him what he craved.

I'd tell Carl's story. I wouldn't use my former roommate's real name, but his downward spiral, as I'd observed it, was a tale Reed would relish. Alcohol and academics. The good gone bad. Dreams and aspirations crushed. Reed would find Carl's sad story immensely fulfilling, maybe even exhilarating.

Back in my room, I was sketching out a few ideas when Tindall walked in and handed me an essay he'd submitted in Dr. Howell's English 111. The composition, which ran 1,500 words, described a summer day at Rehoboth Beach, Delaware, where Tindall worked while in high school, renting beach umbrellas to bathers who had come to enjoy the sun and salt air. As the beachgoers lounge beneath their colorful cloth canopies, a thunderstorm rolls in from the ocean, and the first-person narrator must scurry to collect the umbrellas before they tumble into the roiling surf.

Tindall had gotten the descriptions just right: the dark cascading clouds, the wind and thunder, the human stampede from the beach to the boardwalk and shelter. And he'd managed to incorporate a few poetic touches that enlivened and illuminated his prose. It was the perfect essay, chock-full of images that brought the narrative to life. He'd received an A on the paper.

"This is great!" I said. "How'd you get the idea?"

"I wrote what I knew," he said, repeating the admonition of every creative writing teacher who ever taught a class of dunderheads.

I was inspired. I sat down at my portable Olivetti typewriter and banged out the title: "The Making of a Derelict." I wrote three paragraphs describing my first night at Elon and Carl's lengthy discourse on all he expected to achieve at college—the class presidency, his half-baked marriage plans, and his determination to major in German when the college offered no such major. I worked deliberately, carefully checking my punctuation with my *Harbrace*, and I made good progress until I reached the bottom of the first page, at which point my inspiration waned, and I hit a wall. I wrote out in longhand five or six possible transitional sentences, but none of them seemed to fit with what I'd written thus far. After enumerating Carl's laughable aspirations, I couldn't get myself to the next passage in the essay. Moreover, my words, strung haphazardly together, lacked pizzazz. How could I get myself fired up again? I took a break and dropped in on Witt Halle.

"Do you still have that copy of *Last Exit to Brooklyn*?" I asked.

"Sure do," Witt said. "You want it?"

"Read me the section with Tralala in it."

"Read it yourself," Witt said, tossing me the paperback.

I hurried back to my room and read *Last Exit* for an hour. It was scary stuff—rapes and gang fights and murders—but it occurred to me that I might be able to write something that projected as much energy as Hubert Selby had compressed into his prose. All I had to do was create characters who would talk like people talk. They didn't have to use obscene language, but they could say what real human beings say in real situations. I put *Last Exit* aside and inserted more dialogue in my essay, quoting from the conversations I'd had with Carl.

I began to exaggerate, emphasizing selective elements of Carl's story so they'd be more memorable, and cutting any particulars that didn't nudge the narrative along. I described the pile of dirty laundry, the collection of colognes that was sold off bottle by bottle for beer money, the skipped classes, the late nights spent carousing, the mornings Carl slept till noon, and his mawkish hangovers. As I approached the essay's conclusion, I had Carl packing his bags and departing for home, leaving behind the wreckage of his hopes and dreams. I ended the essay with a zinger straight from Grandmother Drager: "No doubt, psychologists can give you all kinds of reasons for Carl's lack of success, but I'm inclined to place my reliance in the adage: 'A good man gone wrong is a bad man found out.'" Her suggestion regarding tennis shoes may have been ludicrous, but her favorite maxim sure came in handy.

I finished the first draft late that afternoon and went to dinner believing I'd produced a significant piece of writing. As I cleaned up the pots and pans in the back of the cafeteria, I repeated passages from memory and dreamed up scenes that might improve the plot. I wasn't the least bothered by the fact that hardly any of the details in my final draft were true. As far as I knew, Carl was still bunking in our old room. Maybe he was attending classes and doing well, or well enough. I'd passed him once or twice on my way to class and we exchanged pleasantries, so he was hanging on, however tenuously. But I wasn't concerned with the truth. I needed a good grade in English 111, and I was prepared to offer up the ravaged, decaying carcass of my former roommate if that's what the assignment required.

That might have been the end of it—I might have made a few revisions and handed in the essay without giving it more thought—but I was so terrified of Tully Reed that I read the essay over when I awakened the following morning, and discovered, much to my chagrin, that it was horrible. A piece of trash. An F for sure. I was dazed by my utter lack of competence. Since I didn't have an alternative topic and I'd already expended four or five hours on my essay, I set about rewriting what I'd committed to paper. I went through the composition line by line, asking myself if I could make each sentence better than it was. Usually, I could. I'd work for an hour or so and then put the essay aside. I kept up with the assignments for my other classes, but each afternoon I'd make revisions and corrections to my essay. At night I'd crawl into bed and review in my mind various passages that needed improving. Ideas came to me each morning in the shower, and for the next three days, I labored over the text until it was as good as I could get it. Then I sat down and retyped my creation on erasable bond, carefully rubbing out my typos, making the corrections and inserting minor improvements. A fair copy in hand, I hurried to class on the designated day and handed my first college essay to the scariest teacher who'd ever terrified a classroom full of fuzzballs.

That little essay—it wasn't more than 1,800 words—had occupied six days of my life, but I believed I had a shot at a decent grade. Since Reed didn't say when he might return the essays, I tried to put it out of my mind. We had no other pending assignments in his class, so I figured a large part of my final grade would be based on my essay—and of course the final exam, whatever that might be.

A week passed. At night my essay appeared like an apparition in my dreams, and I'd awaken believing I'd omitted a crucial word in a strategic paragraph, or that I'd made a subject-verb or pronoun error or I'd written a stupidly convoluted sentence. Then I'd toss and turn the rest of the night.

As was my habit, I dropped by the library in the Carlton Building on Wednesday evening after working in the cafeteria so I could read *Newsweek* and *Time*. There was a TV on second Smith, but the owner charged a dollar an hour to watch it, so my knowledge of world events came almost exclusively from weekly news magazines and what I heard on WBAG, which wasn't much. Reed's office was on the second floor of Carlton, and after perusing *Newsweek*, I sneaked past his door to see if he might be grading papers. He wasn't. His office was always dark, at least when I was in the building, and I began to suspect that he might never return our essays.

"I've graded your papers," Reed announced at the end of class on November 19, "and the grades were what I expected." He marched down the aisle calling out our surnames. When a student raised his or her hand, an essay was sent flying in that general direction and fluttered to the floor if the recipient wasn't quick enough to snatch it in midair. Flashes of red ink were visible for all to see. In a few cases I caught a glimpse of the grades—Ds and Fs, mostly. I was on the edge of regurgitating my grits when Reed called out "Smith!" I raised my hand and my precious essay sailed like a paper airplane in my direction. I was up and grabbed it in a nanosecond. I staggered backward, feeling for my seat with my free hand before collapsing into the pew.

A bold red C- was scrawled above my clever title. There were no other red marks on the first and second pages, and when I turned to the third page, a big "Good!" was scribbled in the margin beside the line: ". . . but I'm inclined to place my reliance in the old adage: 'A good man gone wrong is a bad man found out.'"

C-? What the hell? Reed hadn't marked any grammar, punctuation, or spelling errors, and he had commended me for my clever conclusion. How'd I get a C-? It was the lowest grade I'd received so far at Elon.

"Any questions?" he asked after returning our papers, but none of us dared to make a public inquiry. I hurried back to my room and sat at my desk reading over "The Making of a Derelict." Regardless of the grade I'd received, I thought my essay pretty heady stuff! After reading through it once, I read it a second and third time, and with each reading I grew angrier. I was the best writer in the class, and I'd gotten a miserable C-. Impossible!

I stewed for a few days, awakening in the middle of the night—it was beginning to be a worrisome habit—to ponder what I might do to have Reed change my grade for the better. Should I try to talk with him after class? Probably not. He was usually in a hurry to make his escape. I didn't want to aggravate him. He might change my grade to an F. On the other hand, he'd likely think better of me if I took the time to inquire as to why I'd received a C-. I wanted to believe a face-to-face encounter would go down like this:

"Professor Reed, may I ask you a question?"

"Certainly," he'd say, "I'm happy to answer student questions."

"Well, I was wondering why I got a C- on my essay. The only mark on my paper, other than the grade, was the word 'Good!' in the margin beside my last sentence."

I'd hand the paper to Reed, who'd stare at my masterpiece and say, "Why, this is obviously a mistake. I'm pleased you took the time to bring this to my attention. You deserve an A... no, because you took the initiative to seek me out, I'll make it an A+."

It also occurred to me that it might go the other way. He'd say, "You haven't taken a critical look at your writing, and since you decided to bother me with your trifling problem, I'll change the grade to an F . . . no, I'll change it to an F-. How's that?"

On the Thursday afternoon following the return of my essay, I happened by Reed's office and, wonder of wonders, the light was on and the door was ajar. He was sitting ramrod-straight behind his desk smoking a cigarette and scribbling hurriedly on student papers with a fat red pen. I paused to consider whether to interrupt him, but I had my notebook with me, and my essay was carefully tucked inside. I took a deep breath and knocked on the door molding.

"What do you want?" he snapped, swiveling in his chair to look me in the eye.

"I have a question concerning my essay?"

"You have it with you?"

"Yes, sir."

"All right, come in."

I pulled the folded essay out of my notebook and handed it to him. He scanned the first page, flipped to the second and then the third.

"What class are you in?" he asked.

"Your 8 o'clock 111 . . . and I was wondering why I got a C-. There are no mistakes marked on the paper."

He stared at me over his tortoiseshell reading glasses. "Your essay's fine, no spelling, punctuation, or grammar errors. You got the highest grade in the class. You ought to be pleased."

"Was there something wrong with the content?"

"Not really. And your conclusion was good."

"Oh," I said. "I was wondering—"

"It's not A or B work," he said, shaking his head, "not for a college freshman." He handed me my essay, took a drag on his Lucky Strike and returned to slinging red ink.

The essay I'd slaved and agonized over for days was of no particular interest to Reed—it was another stupid paper by another stupid freshman. An annoyance. A banality. And he was right: I was lucky to have gotten a C-.

I walked back to my room and stuffed "The Making of a Derelict" into my desk drawer, determined to forget it once and for all. Although I didn't realize it at the time, the experience revealed to me what I'd have to endure to write an acceptable college essay.

# Nine

"I've got an idea," Tindall said. "Let's hitch to Boone."

We'd hit the freshman slump, the lull between Thanksgiving and Christmas. Everyone on second Smith had grown apathetic. The Christmas break was two weeks away, exams were a month and a half off, scheduled for late January, and most of our coursework was behind us. We'd grown weary of the Tap Room, the B&B Smoke Shop, and kicking around downtown Burlington. So, we'd gathered in my dorm room for a pre-weekend bull session. Maynard and Scott, slouched on Brinkley's bunk with their backs pressed to the beige cinderblock wall, stared at Tindall as he spoke. I leaned forward in my desk chair.

"Boone?" Gene asked. "Why in heaven's name would you want to hitch to Boone? Doesn't sound like a good way to spend the weekend."

"Let's do something," Tindall said, "even if it's stupid."

I piped in: "I'll go with you."

"You guys are nuts," Scott said. "You'll end up standing on the side of the highway like when I picked you up in Richmond."

Based as it was on my recent hitchhiking disaster, Scott's prediction was mildly persuasive, but I'd caught the travel bug and it hadn't yet occurred to me that begging rides from strangers might be dangerous.

"It'll be a piece of cake," Tindall said. "Boone is just far enough away to make the trip interesting."

I'd survived the I-95 debacle, so thumbing on I-85 didn't strike me as particularly problematic. I-85 lacked "No Hitchhiking" signs, and the impediments facing us on a trip to Boone weren't as daunting as those I'd encountered on my Maryland outing. I wouldn't be traveling alone—Tindall and I would be on the buddy system—and Boone was only slightly more than half the distance from Burlington to Annapolis.

"You guys are crazy," Gene said.

"I looked at a map and after we get past Winston-Salem, it's mostly hick towns and back roads," Tindall said. "Country folk love to pick up college kids. Makes them feel like they're doing a good deed, you know, making the world a better place."

"I'm in," I said, reinforcing my earlier commitment.

I'd never visited the North Carolina mountains, and I longed to hear real fiddlers and banjo pickers who could sing in that whiny nasal twang that's so essential to the authentic rendering of "Wildwood Flower" and "Shady Grove." I imagined they'd be like the Darlings on *The Andy Griffith Show*, Briscoe and Charlene ingenuous and outgoing and "the boys" lacking even a trace of natural energy but likely to break into an old-timey tune at the least provocation. If Tindall and I happened to hitch a ride in a bootlegger's souped-up coupé like the one Robert Mitchum drove in *Thunder Road*, all the better. Powersliding into a tight mountain switchback in a '40 Ford propelled by a bored-and-stroked 331 Chrysler Hemi with two four barrels and a hundred gallons of tangle-leg onboard struck me as the ultimate Southern adventure.

Tindall nailed it down: "All right, it's decided."

That's when someone in our little coterie brought up the possibility of meeting girls. "That place is crawling with women" was the statement that caught my attention.

We may have been ineffectual freshmen living a tiresome cliché, but we weren't without wit, and the mere mention of women caused us to lapse into self-parody. Anyone overhearing the conversation would have assumed that Appalachian State was little more than an enormous brothel with only enough men on campus to field football and basketball teams, and not very good ones at that.

Maynard piped in, "I bet you could walk into any girls' dorm, phone up to one of the floors and ask if there are a couple of Daisy Maes who want to date two good-looking studs. You'd have your pick of the best-looking women on campus. Just tell them you're pre-med students at Chapel Hill."

Gene caught on immediately. "Yeah," he added sarcastically, "those Appalachian chicks will be all over you guys."

So Tindall and I agreed: We would undertake the Last Great Freshman Road Trip, an utterly frivolous enterprise with its roots deep in the college experience. The conventions of such a journey would later be immortalized in popular film, but what we had planned was the road trip in its most elemental form. No big black Lincoln Continental. No deep pockets stuffed with twenty-dollar bills. We would set off the following afternoon, our thumbs out, our pockets empty, our souls unsullied, and we'd let the chips fall where they may.

Boone was, in those days, a four-hour drive from Burlington. If we departed after Saturday classes, we might arrive at Appalachian State by 6 p.m., giving us plenty of time to get imaginary dates with imaginary women who'd spent their imaginary lives awaiting our arrival.

After my Saturday political science class, I hurried back to the second floor of Smith and found Tindall waiting. "Ready to hit the road?" I asked.

"Let's go," he said.

And we were on our way, traveling light, the clothes on our backs—button-down Oxford shirts, crew-neck sweaters, corduroy jeans, sand-colored desert boots and wool car coats, our colorful scarves hanging loose around the collars, evidence that we were cool guys from mysterious milieus north of the Virginia mudflats. We didn't bother with blanket rolls. In theory, we'd be enjoying a passionate night with the grateful women who took us in, so we need not drag along useless trappings.

Timing was crucial. If we didn't make it to Boone in five or six hours, the sun would set, and our chances of catching rides beyond the point where we were deposited would be greatly diminished. Nobody, good intentions notwithstanding, was going to pick up a couple of numbskulls standing in the dark on the side of a country road. If stranded, our lack of funds—together we had enough cash to pay the cover charge at a dance club, if we found one—would make it impossible for us to get a motel room or buy ourselves an adequate dinner or breakfast. But no matter, it was a cool, clear, blue Saturday in late November, and we were willing to leave our immediate disposition to fate.

At 12:15 p.m. Tindall and I were strategically positioned in front of the Sigma Mu house on Williamson Avenue with our thumbs out. We weren't there more than a minute when Dr. Cates, a sociology professor, slowed his car to a stop and reached across the front seat to open the passenger-side door for Tindall. I slid into the back seat, which was cluttered with textbooks and piles of folded student papers secured with rubber bands.

"Where are you boys going?" Cates asked.

"I-85," I said, "and then to the mountains."

We would never have guessed that Cates would give us a ride. A thin avuncular man with wire spectacles sliding down his pinched nose, he was known to be shyer than a unicorn. He might have thought we were students in one of his classes, but it was more likely he gave us a ride because we *weren't* his students, and he recognized us as familiar strangers from the campus. Whatever his motivation, he seemed relieved that his contribution to our trip would be brief.

"The mountains, huh?" he asked.

"We're getting away for the weekend," Tindall said.

"That's a long way to hitchhike," Cates said.

That's when I began to have doubts concerning our impending journey. It was one thing for the guys in the dorm to question the wisdom of our undertaking, but when an honest-to-God Ph.D. expressed misgivings, it might be time to reconsider. Still, I couldn't back out unless Tindall agreed to do the same. If the guys on second Smith heard that I'd turned chicken, I'd never hear the end of it.

Cates dropped us at the Burlington city limits. He wished us good luck, and we scrambled onto the shoulder of I-85 South. I was about to voice my reservations, suggesting that we catch a ride to the Tap Room, when a late-model Chevy station wagon pulled over and spirited us through Greensboro and Winston-Salem and onto N.C. 421. We hadn't even stuck out our thumbs, and we'd gotten a ride that took us a good hundred miles from Burlington.

The driver was a bald, obese salesman headed to Boone to visit his son who was, he said, a junior on the verge of flunking out. "I'm going to lay down the law," he said. "I'm out here day in and day out working my fingers to the bone, and he's up there sleeping in till noon and partying all weekend. That, I can assure you, is going to change—and I mean right now...." He continued to rail about his dead-end job, his ungrateful wife, his shiftless son, and the terrible hand life had dealt him. Safely stashed in the back seat, I eventually had to roll down my window halfway so the wind would drown out the endless carping.

As we traveled westward, the temperature dropped into the mid-50s, and the mountains rose dark on the horizon. I'd visited the Skyline Drive, sanitized with its overlooks and fancy campgrounds, with my family, and we'd traveled the Pennsylvania Turnpike into the Alleghenies on our way to visit my father's family in Ohio, so I could feign a passing knowledge of the high country. But other than log cabins perched precariously on boulder-strewn mountainsides and banjos roiling in fog-shrouded hollers, I had no idea what to expect in what I mistakenly thought of as the Great Smokies.

The road to Boone was a new world of rolling countryside dotted with white clapboard churches, dilapidated mom-and-pop groceries, and burned-out mobile homes encircled by abandoned truck bodies and spent refrigerators. Road signs for Millers Creek, Mulberry, and Deep Gap flickered by. We passed under a granite overpass on the Blue Ridge Parkway, twisted into Watauga County, and with dusk gathering, we made the Boone city limits. The trip had taken four and a half hours.

Our ride skirted the university with its high-rise brick dorms and imposing administration and classroom buildings and deposited us in front of a convenience store at the edge of town. "I'm going to have to drop you boys here," the salesman said. "You don't want to be around when I find my kid. It ain't gonna be pretty."

The evening sky was a smear of gauzy watercolors, crimson streaked with gray, gold, and blue. Predictably, there was no sign of the randy co-eds who were supposed to greet us with a torchlight procession, so we checked out the convenience store hoping to buy a bottle of cheap wine. When we asked the clerk where the alcoholic beverages were shelved, he laughed. "Boone is dry," he said. "There's no beer or nothing here." Which, like so many things in the South, made no sense. Where did the thousands of thirsty Appalachian students get their buzz?

"Is there someplace close where we can buy some wine?" Tindall asked.

"Blowing Rock," the clerk said. "It's ten miles from here."

We were immediately on the road again, headed into the mountains that rose steeply all around us. If we couldn't hook up with females—that had, after all, *never* been a possibility—we could at least get a little drunk. But it was dark, and the drivers of passing cars increased their speed as they approached the curve where we were standing. After waiting another hour, a cigar-smoking mechanic in greasy coveralls and a mangled porkpie hat pulled over in his '59 Ford and drove us into Blowing Rock. He dropped us at another convenience store, where we bought a bottle of Napa Sonoma Mendocino red for eighty-nine cents, a loaf of Wonder Bread for a quarter, and a package of American cheese for thirty cents. At least we'd have something to eat and drink.

Back on the shoulder of the road with our provender, our mountain adventure began to degenerate into outright fiasco. As we waited for one last ride to take us wherever we were going, we cracked nervous jokes that only emphasized our stupidity. "Look, is that a carload of girls I see headed our way?" or "What do you say we go to the bar in the Hilton for a beer before we check in?" I had no idea where we were, and I didn't have more than a dollar in change in my pocket. I suspected Tindall had a plan. Maybe he had Delaware friends who lived in the mountains and they'd put us up for the night. Failing that, I hoped he had a few bucks he hadn't mentioned so we could get a room and buy a real dinner. Perhaps he suspected the same of me. For an hour or so we waited, hoping someone would take pity on two stranded hitchhikers.

"We might be standing here all night," Tindall observed.

"Yeah," I agreed, feeling forsaken. "Maybe we should have thought of this before we left the dorm."

"Having no plan is the whole point," Tindall said. "It wouldn't be any fun if we knew what we were doing."

"I get it," I said. But I didn't.

The temperature was dropping rapidly, our breath vaporizing as we spoke. It was going to be a long, cold night, not unlike the evening I'd endured south of Richmond—but colder and longer and with no hope of rescue. Scott, Gene, and Maynard were safe and warm at the Tap Room, drinking Blue Ribbons and eating pickled eggs while we waited in the darkness for a brakeless tractor-trailer truck to smear us across the asphalt. But there was nothing we could do but keep on hitching, even if we had no destination.

Our last ride of the evening, a '50s pickup truck, pulled over at 8:30 p.m. Inside the warm cab, Tindall asked the driver, a terse middle-aged man decked out in a cheap three-piece suit and a sweat-stained ball cap, his lower lip ripe with snuff, how far it was to Grandfather Mountain.

"It's a good ways," he said. "I ain't going all the way to Grandfather Mountain, but I can drop you nearby." In our pre-departure discussion, Tindall hadn't mentioned Grandfather Mountain, and I'd never heard of the place, so maybe he had a plan after all. Perhaps there were cabins open to college kids who found themselves lost in this mysterious country. Probably there was food—plates of beef stew full of vegetables—and friendly females anxious for a good time. But when the driver left us on an even more remote stretch of highway far away from any signs of civilization, I lost all hope.

"Well, what should we do now?" I asked as we watched the

single taillight of the truck dissolve into grim finality.

"I guess we'd better find a place to camp," Tindall suggested.

"Where?"

"Let's go up on the side of that mountain. Maybe there's a campsite or a cabin or something like that."

We scrambled up an escarpment, the rocky earth crumbling beneath our feet as we struggled higher. As we left the empty, silent road far behind, the woods grew denser and darker. Lights from faraway dwellings winked on distant mountainsides. When we reached what seemed to be a precipice, we backtracked into the woods until we found a boulder overhang that promised a slight degree of shelter.

"Let's have something to eat," I suggested.

"Yeah, this looks like a good place to camp," Tindall said.

The clearing was nearly flat, cushioned with decaying leaves. We sat down, twisted open the screw-top Napa Sonoma Mendocino red, and made cheese sandwiches. We drank straight from the bottle, passing it back and forth. After a few healthy swigs, I accepted that we had reached our destination. I stared into the wooded darkness and asked, "Are there bears around here?"

"Bears! There are no bears in these mountains."

"Yeah, well, where do they live?"

"I don't know," he answered. "Maybe in the Rocky Mountains. There are too many people around here. Bears are scared of people."

"They are? I never heard that. Who says they're scared of people? They eat people, don't they?" I stared off into the impenetrable darkness, listening for the sound of a 700-pound grizzly crunching through the woods. "People get eaten by bears all the time," I continued, "and bears live in these woods, and they eat dumbasses like us if they're hungry enough."

Tindall looked around. "Maybe one of us should stay awake,"

he suggested.

"Yeah, maybe."

Discussing the proximity of ravenous grizzlies wasn't doing us any good, so I changed the subject. "I can see the guys at the Tap Room drinking beer and having a high ole time." I meant my observation to be wistful, but Tindall took it as sarcasm.

"Yeah, they're probably bored to death and wishing they'd come with us."

His misapprehension made me laugh. We were in the middle of nowhere, with no protection against the cold but our thin coats and wool scarves. Unpleasant carnivores lurked in the mysterious darkness, waiting to charge into our camp to rip us to pieces. I pulled the wool hood of my car coat over my head and wrapped my scarf tightly around my neck. "You know, we should have brought some matches. We could have started a fire."

"We'd probably have set the entire mountainside on fire. Then we'd get arrested."

"Locked up in a warm jail doesn't sound so bad right now."

The wine buzz was growing warmer, so I curled up in the fetal position and gradually drifted off to sleep. And I slept amazingly well, considering the rocky ground, the temperature, which must have dropped into the upper 30s, and the threat posed by wild animals. I stirred once or twice during the night, wondered where I was, stared into the starry heavens, and reflected on the miscalculations that had landed me in this situation. What had happened to my good sense? I should have anticipated our present circumstance. I should have brought a blanket and borrowed a couple of bucks from one of the guys. But there was no benefit in taking myself to task. I squeezed my eyes shut, sucked in a deep breath of cold mountain air, and told myself that things could be worse, although I couldn't, at that moment, imagine how.

∴

When I woke in the gray light of morning, Tindall was still asleep, curled around a tree trunk with his back to me. I sat up and scanned the woods and boulders that surrounded us. In the early morning light, our campsite had undergone a transformation. What we thought was a well-protected location in the lee of an outcropping was no more than a nondescript clearing in the middle of an ordinary patch of woodland. The ledge under which we'd slept was a boulder protruding from the mountainside. Through the bare branches of hardwoods—the leaves had long since drifted to earth—I could see a brown valley that stretched around the base of the mountain. An ancient creek flowed through the bottom of a gorge, and sections of serpentine road eased up the valley and twisted into the countryside.

Tindall sat up and rubbed his eyes. We stretched our legs and collected our wits and then, without exchanging a word, we took off running, careening down the mountainside as fast as our legs could carry us, plunging headlong toward the winding highway below. It was all I could do to keep my legs under me, but I was enjoying the surge of full gallop charge when I heard Tindall scream, "Jesus!"

From the corner of my eye, I saw him slide into the loamy earth with one leg extended as if he were stealing second base—and I managed to stop inches from the edge of a sheer cliff over which I'd almost plummeted. We both teetered there for an instant, looking downward in horror.

"Jesus!" I echoed.

We sidestepped along the cliff and descended into a deep, rocky ravine that eventually led back to N.C. 221. The road was deserted that Sunday morning, and we had to wait an hour to catch a ride into Burke County to a crossroads occupied by a paint-bare country store patched with soda and tobacco signs and crowned with a rusting red and white *Coca-Cola* button. When we opened the creaking door, I expected to see a bevy of hawk-faced country folk gathered around a potbellied stove, but there was only a wizened, gray-bearded man in bib overalls, and a mousy pubescent girl. Blue-eyed, chinless and dangerously thin, she was slump shouldered in a faded green print dress and a yellow sweater buttoned tight below her budding breasts. Her hair was dull brown and stringy, and she bore a sickly resemblance to Sarah Jean, my Burlington date who turned out to be preggers. But this girl seemed genuinely glad to see us and smiled, displaying a mouthful of ruined teeth.

"Hey, boys!" she said gleefully.

"What can I get for y'all?" the old man asked.

"I'll have some nabs?" Tindall said, sliding a quarter across the counter.

I dug deep into my coat pocket, retrieved my remaining change and cranked two sodas from the moldy cooler by the door. I marveled at the array of campy items neatly arranged on the shelves behind the well-worn wood-topped counter—canned goods of all sorts (Negro Head Oysters caught my attention), red bandannas and cheap handkerchiefs, the obligatory Moon Pies, and work gloves. A couple of decomposing, cloth-shrouded country hams hung from the rafters, and tins of sardines were stacked high on a shelf above the proprietor's head. On the countertop lay a Diamond Dust punch card decorated with the names of baseball players from the 1930s—Travis Jackson, Pie Traynor, Lou Gehrig, Babe Ruth—guys I'd heard my father brag on. Attached to the thick punch board was a frayed string anchoring a slender wooden dowel. There were hundreds of punches. "5¢ Each" was printed in the corner of the board.

"Try your luck?" the proprietor suggested.

"How's it work?" I asked.

"Ya use this little stick here to push out one of them holes and a piece of paper comes out the other side to tell ya if you're a winner. Ya might win ten bucks."

After buying the sodas, I had two quarters in my pocket, but Tindall had a few nickels left over from our visit to the convenience store in Blowing Rock. He pushed one of the nickels across the countertop with his index finger and the old man deposited it in the chest pocket of his overalls. The grinning girl sidled in close to observe the results of Tindall's high-stakes gamble.

I was hopeful—we'd lived through the night, hadn't we?—and I was sure Tindall would hit the jackpot. We'd soon be chowing down on big plates of eggs, bacon, and grits at a restaurant on the highway. He carefully pushed the tiny scrolled paper out the backside of the board, and using his thumb and forefinger, unrolled it on the countertop.

"It's a loser," Tindall said. "There's a surprise."

"Ya wanna try again?" the old man asked.

"That'll do it for me," Tindall replied.

"Some guy won five dollars the other day," the girl said. "If you win, Granddaddy's gotta give you the money."

"I appreciate it," Tindall said, "but I've had enough."

We finished our sodas and nabs, and Tindall asked for directions to the nearest interstate. The old man suggested we hitch to Lenoir, where we would pick up I-85 north. "It's thirty miles," he said, pointing through the screen door and into the distance where the blacktop twisted skyward. We thanked the old man and his granddaughter and she smiled, her teeth all awry like a busted-up picket fence.

While we waited on the shoulder of the road, I laughed as

Tindall mocked the poor country girl. He was a master of mimicry, conjuring up impersonations at will, most of them based loosely on movie clichés.

"Please take me with you," he mocked. "I don't wanna stay here for the rest of my life. Won't you city fellas please take me with you, please, please. I've got rickets and a tapeworm and I've gotta get outta here."

I looked back at the storefront and glimpsed the girl staring at us through a grimy windowpane. She smiled and waved. I waved back.

We caught a ride in a Volkswagen driven by a chatty tourist from Pennsylvania. Well into another blue Carolina day, the road south took us through hick towns populated with churchgoers driving fifteen miles per hour in old blue and white Ford and Chevy pickups, their cargo beds brimming with sullen children and the occasional bluetick hound sniffing the morning air. We caught a ride north on I-85 with a couple of guys from Wake Forest, and as soon as they dropped us on the outskirts of Winston-Salem, miracle of miracles, a blonde in a red Corvette convertible with the top down pulled onto the shoulder and yelled, "Jump in!"—which we did without hesitation.

"Where you boys going?" she asked. Her blond hair was wind-tangled and glistened in the afternoon sun. She was the first college-age woman who had spoken a friendly word to me since I'd set foot in North Carolina, and I marveled at her blue eyes and broad smile, which was genuine and wholly disarming. Our luck was changing for the better.

"Burlington," I said. "We sure appreciate the lift."

Tindall quickly slid in next to the blonde, and he immediately slipped his arm around the back of her seat. I squeezed in between the passenger-side door and Tindall. She dropped the Vette in

Tindall answered. "She was driving a Vette with the top down and she gave us a ride."

Tindall supplied the narrative line, backing up here and there to flesh out our adventure. I added occasional embroidery, and gradually the story began to take on a bright, three-dimensional form that kept our envious listeners spellbound. Tindall's version of events didn't quite jive with mine, but I didn't contradict him. We took no credit for sexual conquests—no sane person was buying into that malarkey—but the drivers who picked us up were supremely interesting, and the sunset was a spectacular canvas of blues, reds, and gray. The woods in which we camped were darker and scarier than belief. The wine was tastier, the cheese (French, not American) was riper, and the Wonder Bread acquired the crusty tastiness of a baguette. The cliff we'd narrowly avoided plummeting over was higher than I remembered, and the girl at the country store was charmingly seductive and wanted nothing more than to be swept away by the handsome strangers who had happened into her lonely, thwarted life. Her expressive, liquid eyes begged us to rescue her. But brutes that we were, we abandoned her to live out her days among the hayseeds.

If no one had been interested in hearing my Richmond hitchhiking tale, harrowing as it was, the account of our mountain adventure kept the guys enthralled. Tindall's meticulous descriptions, his use of humor, and the inclusion of carefully selected details, enhanced though they may have been, were immediately accepted as Gospel. I marveled at his cinematic storytelling. By the time he'd finished his account of our weekend adventure, we were honest-to-God heroes.

gear, scratched onto the asphalt and we headed east, happy as any three humans could be, shoehorned as we were into a two-seater.

A beach-music station was cranked up full volume, and we jived the forty miles back to Alamance County to the strains of the Tams, Willie Tee, the Dominoes. We couldn't talk with our beautiful benefactor—there was too much wind and road noise and the radio was maxed out—but her mere presence was exhilarating, intoxicating. I was in love for sure and was heartbroken when she dropped us on the shoulder of the interstate at the very spot where we'd begun our trip twenty-six hours before. I sighed as she pulled into traffic and vanished in a haze of blue exhaust.

"I wish the guys in the dorm had been here to see us climb out of that Vette," Tindall said.

It was midafternoon when we clambered up the steps to the second floor of Smith. Tindall headed to his room, and I flopped down on my bed for a little well-deserved rest. As usual, Brinkley had gone home to Zuni for the weekend and the room was blessedly quiet. I dozed for an hour.

When I awakened, I shed my gamey clothes—I was none too fresh after two days on the road and a night sleeping under the stars—and I danced in a long, hot shower, brushed my teeth, and shaved. Decked out in clean cords and a white shirt, I hurried down to Tindall's room, where Witt, Gene, Scott and Maynard had gathered to hear the story of our epic journey. Tindall was holding forth.

"Turns out you can't buy wine or beer in Boone," he was saying as I walked into the room.

"I could have told you that," Gene said. "A lot of those mountain counties don't sell alcohol. They make their own in the woods."

Maynard asked, "Did you meet any women?"

"We met the best-looking blonde you've ever laid eyes on,"

# Ten

"Get up! Get up! Get up, up, up!" my mother blurted. It was at 6:30 a.m., the first day of Christmas break, and as always she felt compelled to rouse her children at the most ungodly hour. I lifted my head from the pillow and stared bleary-eyed at her figure in the bedroom doorway. Wrapped to her chin in a blue terry cloth robe, her fists were planted firmly on her hips. She meant business. "You're to march yourself down to the Safeway and ask Mr. Short if he'll give you a job for the holidays," she ordered. "You can earn enough money to pay for your books next semester. And next time I see Mr. Short, I'll find out if you asked him for a job."

"Can't you even say, 'Welcome home'?" I asked.

"Sure. Welcome home, Mr. Big Shot College Guy. Now get out of that bed and get yourself down to the Safeway."

I was suffering from severe sleep deprivation. I'd caught an all-night ride home from North Carolina and had dragged into the house on Janice Drive at 3:15 a.m. But my mother was not to be denied, so I managed to pull on the wrinkled clothes I'd worn the day before and stumbled downstairs to eat a bowl of my brother's Froot Loops. At 8:30 a.m. I scuffled up Bay Ridge Avenue to the Eastport Shopping Center, where I found Mr. Short on the dock, supervising the unloading of pallets of dog food from a tractor trailer. He shook my hand and asked how college was going.

"It's fine," I answered. "I was hoping you might have an opening for a cashier during the holidays. I'm not looking to work eight hours a day, but, you know, something part time."

"If I had an opening, I'd hire you," he said. "But right now I have all the cashiers I need. I'd have to cut someone else's hours, and that wouldn't be fair, especially at Christmas." My spirits soared. If he didn't have an opening, I could pass the holidays stretched out on my bed reading P.G. Wodehouse. "I'll tell you what," he continued. "I've got a friend who's the manager at the Drug Fair in Parole. Go see him and tell him I sent you. He's looking for holiday help."

A job at Drug Fair was the last thing I wanted, but I had to make an inquiry. My mother was as good as her word, and I knew she'd buttonhole Mr. Short the next time she visited the Safeway. If she found out I hadn't applied for the Drug Fair job, she'd make my Christmas break miserable, which she had already begun to do by waking me before sunup.

Among cashiers, there existed a hierarchy, and working a register at Safeway carried with it a degree of status and a wage that was at least $1.75 an hour. Drug Fair was a discount pharmacy, emporium and grocery store, a low-rent warehouse for plastic crap and wilted vegetables, where the discount prices were clearly marked on each item—work for the dimwitted—and the pay was $1.25 an hour.

I caught the bus to Parole and found the Drug Fair manager, a rumpled, balding, ectomorphic fellow with thick wire spectacles and a long pointy nose, puzzling over paperwork in an elevated office that overlooked a line of disheveled employees who were pounding away at their cash registers. He appeared to be in emotional distress, his mouth screwed into a grotesque snarl.

"Excuse me," I said.

He looked up, snatched the glasses from his face and tossed them on the countertop in a display of frustration. "Mr. Short over at Safeway said I should talk with you about working as a cashier for the holidays. I don't need a full-time job, just some part-time work if you've got it."

Sweet relief swept over his face, his lips stretching into a half smile. "Mr. Short sent you?" he asked.

"He said you might need an experienced cashier."

"You used to work at the Safeway?"

"For two years, until I went off to college."

He grinned fully. I was apparently the man he'd been waiting for. He stepped out of his office, planted both feet flat on the linoleum and looked me up and down. "Can you work a register?" he asked.

"Yes, sir."

"And you've worked stock?"

"Yes, sir."

My God, he was going to hire me! I was going to spend the next two weeks checking out Christmas junk at the Drug Fair for minimum wage! This was not good.

The manager handed me a pen and an application clamped to a clipboard, and I took a couple of minutes to fill in the information.

"Follow me," he said, and we walked quickly down aisle four toward the back of the crowded store. "I can use you to relieve my regular cashiers for their lunch and supper breaks, and you can help keep the shelves stocked, especially this display. We're selling the hell out of these things." He pointed to a chest-high pyramid of black, orange and beige boxes crowned with an unboxed white plastic kitchen device known to every American who owned a TV. "We've had to restock this display three times this morning. You know anything about these Veg-O-Matics?" he asked.

What happened next was probably brought on by fatigue—or maybe I needed an excuse to get fired before I got hired. Whatever the cause, a synaptic misfire propelled me into the past. I picked up the display device, held it out in front of me and began to deliver the requisite spiel:

"Imagine slicing a whole potato into uniform slices with one motion. Bulk cheese costs less. Look how easy Veg-O-Matic makes many slices at once. Imagine slicing all these radishes in seconds. This is the only appliance in the world that slices whole firm tomatoes in one stroke with every seed in place. Hamburger lovers, feed whole onions into Veg-O-Matic and make these tempting thin slices. Simply turn the dial and change from thin to thick slices. You can slice a whole can of prepared meat at one time. Isn't that amazing? Like magic, change from slicing to dicing. That's right, it slices, it dices, it juliennes, perfect every time!"

By the time I'd finished yammering, the manager's eyes were wide and his jaw slack.

"How'd you learn that?" he asked.

"I used to watch the commercial on TV, and it just sort of stuck in my head."

My fascination with the Veg-O-Matic stretched back to my junior year in high school. Strung out on testosterone and teenage angst, I suffered insomnia for about six months. On those long, restless nights, I'd roll out of bed after everyone else in the house was asleep, slink down to the "rec" room and turn on the black-and-white TV. WJZ, the local CBS affiliate, was the only station out of Baltimore that aired anything other than an Indian Chief test pattern in the early a.m., so I'd tune in channel thirteen in time to catch Father Callahan of St. Francis Xavier House of Prayer bestowing his benediction. Then I'd settle in for a three-hour run of continuous raise-your-own-chinchillas commercials.

My clandestine obsession with Father Callahan and chinchillas continued for two or three months—until the fateful night when the good Father delivered his usual homily and the chinchilla commercials failed to materialize. Instead, a plastic guillotine-like device appeared on the TV screen, contrasted against a background map of the world, below which were printed the words "World Famous Veg-O-Matic." Then a disembodied voice said: "Imagine slicing a whole potato into uniform slices with one motion. Bulk cheese costs less. Look how easy Veg-O-Matic makes many slices at once...."

I'd spent my Father Callahan/chinchilla nights dozing fitfully on the couch and sneaking back to my room before the rest of the family awakened, but on that memorable evening—I've come to think of it as *Night of the Veg-O-Matic*—I sat there stupefied, watching the commercial over and over. I couldn't take my eyes off the screen, and by morning I had the narration memorized—every nuance, modulation and inflection—to which I could add hand gestures, including the graceful upturned palm that beckoned, "Buy me, buy me, buy me...."

Later that day, I was eating lunch in the high school cafeteria with my regular buds when freckle-faced Ronnie Wheeler produced a sliced tomato his mother had wrapped in wax paper to keep it from saturating the white bread he needed to construct his BLT. I jumped up, grabbed the tomato slices and ran through the entire Veg-O-Matic routine, spreading the segments across the Formica tabletop and finishing with the obligatory ". . . perfect every time!"

My friends were speechless, especially Ronnie whose sandwich was ruined. They stared blankly before bursting into hysterics. The vice principal, Mr. Wetherhold, a stern disciplinarian who abhorred any form of frivolity, hurried over to our table to discern the source of the disturbance. "What's going on here?" he asked sternly.

"Do it!" my friends begged. "Do the Veg-O-Matic thing!" They didn't have to ask twice. When I finished my second run-through, it was Mr. Wetherhold who was howling with laughter. Suffice it to say I spent a good deal of my time in high school doing "the Veg-O-Matic thing" for my friends. They never tired of it.

Now the Drug Fair manager's face glowed with approval, and I could see that he'd suffered an epiphany. He rushed into the stockroom and reappeared with a folding table. He extended the legs, positioned the table in front of the pyramid of boxes and covered the top with a square of red cheesecloth. He grabbed an onion from the produce aisle, peeled away the skin, and ordered me to deliver my recitation again, this time with the unboxed Veg-O-Matic at my fingertips.

Despite my long and intimate history with the kitchen device, this was the first time I'd worked with one. But I muddled through the presentation by recalling the images I'd watched hundreds of times on TV, each motion transmitted from memory to physical articulation. I made quick work of the onion, repeating the entire monologue. My demonstration, although clumsy, went well enough to instantly earn me the title: 1965 Parole Drug Fair Veg-O-Matic Man.

"You're hired!" the manager said. "I want you to do a demonstration at the top of every hour. Use all the tomatoes and onions you want but stay away from the cheese and Spam. That stuff costs money."

"Yes, sir," I said dutifully.

"The rest of the time you can restock these Veg-O-Matics

and relieve the cashiers who are going on break. Can you start tomorrow?"

"Yeah," I said. "I guess."

"Be here at 8 o'clock and wear a white shirt."

Crestfallen, I dragged myself into the parking lot and caught the bus back to Eastport. When I stumbled into our living room, it was 11:30 a.m., and I was whipped.

"Did Mr. Short hire you?" my mother yelled from the kitchen.

"He didn't have any openings, but I got a job at Drug Fair in Parole."

"Excellent," she said.

When I turned up at Drug Fair on Saturday morning ready to begin my new career, the manager had anticipated my every need. The folding table was set up in aisle four, which was stocked with kitchen junk—Melmac dishes, spatulas, plastic forks, spoons and knives, etc.—and beside the table waited a freshly replenished pyramid of multicolored boxes containing the Veg-O-Matics. The tabletop was covered with the red cheesecloth from the day before and a white apron of the style that loops around the neck and ties in the back was folded neatly on the table. An unopened can of Spam and a brick of Kraft Velveeta cheese were stacked beside the gleaming white Veg-O-Matic display model I'd used in my earlier demonstration and a bag of assorted vegetables—tomatoes, onions, carrots, and potatoes—awaited their fate. As a touch of class, the manager had placed a roll of paper towels on the table, and a beige commercial dome-topped trash can sat directly behind my workspace.

"Here, wear this," he said, handing me a handsome black clip-on bow tie. I donned my apron and attached the bow tie to the wrinkled collar of my white shirt. "Now show me your stuff.

Just use vegetables. The Spam and cheese are for show."

I launched into my Veg-O-Matic dance at a measured pace, slicing up a small potato and allowing my hands to gracefully execute a lilting swirl at the conclusion of the shtick.

"That was even better than yesterday," the manager beamed, "although I'd take it a little slower if I were you." He looked up and down aisle four. "I'll make an announcement at the top of every hour. You get yourself set up. Sell the hell out of these Veg-O-Matics. If you don't, you'll be in a checkout stand all day." And he left me on my own.

I peeled an onion and trimmed it to the proper size and shape. I was ready. Or as ready as I was ever going to be.

"We are pleased to direct your attention to aisle four," I heard the manager announce over the PA system, "where you can view a demonstration of the miracle Veg-O-Matic, the twentieth century's greatest kitchen appliance. It makes an economical and useful Christmas gift! Do all your Christmas shopping in five minutes and have your Veg-O-Matics gift wrapped right here in the store. Christmas cards are available on aisle six."

After my first two demonstrations, I discovered that operating the Veg-O-Matic wasn't quite the effortless exercise I'd observed on TV. I directed my attention to the tomato, which I positioned perfectly between the upper and lower blades. "This is the only appliance in the world that slices whole firm tomatoes in one stroke with every seed in place," I said, as I slammed down the top of the Veg-O-Matic. The tomato exploded like a water balloon, splattering juice and seeds all over my apron and the tabletop. The two customers who had gathered for my demonstration jumped back and bolted for the exit.

I'd created a huge mess. I mopped the tomato slop off my hands with a paper towel and brushed the seeds from my apron, but pulp continued to dribble from the bottom of the Veg-O-Matic, and I had to retreat to the stockroom to wash the blades. So tomatoes were out. Ripe ones, at least. After mopping the splatter from the tabletop, I attempted to slice an onion I'd peeled earlier. I gave a forceful downward thrust and the device worked perfectly, sending a cascade of onion slivers onto the cheesecloth. Still, it was a messy business; pieces of onion got stuck in the blades and had to be pried out. I had the same experience with carrots, stubborn chunks of which had to be worked free with my fingertips.

I settled, finally, on a peeled Idaho Russet potato. I cut the spud into four pieces, which I fed individually into the chopper. And the device worked as intended—neat and clean. The Veg-O-Matic was, after all, meant to transform a time-consuming, chaotic operation into a simple, wholesome procedure. And that's what it did.

The secret, as with many physical actions, was in the wrist. It was all finesse. I'd place a piece of potato on the bottom blades and apply a sharp downward whack with the top. And voila! The potato was julienned, perfect for hash browns. If I spoke slowly, worked methodically and was meticulous with my cleanup, I could kill the better part of a half hour on each demonstration, thus allowing for only 30 minutes of working at a cash register before my next demonstration.

At first, I was worried that I wouldn't sell enough Veg-O-Matics to keep my new job, but the pile of boxes diminished at an ever-increasing rate as Christmas approached and the manager was a happy man. I'd sold six to eight Veg-O-Matics with each demonstration, and I noticed that many customers who didn't make an immediate purchase returned later to snatch up two or three Veg-O-Matics, having chosen convenience over thoughtful reflection. Usually these return customers felt compelled to offer an explanation for their delayed purchase. "You know," they'd say. "I was thinking about your demonstration, and you're right, this will make an excellent gift for my mother."

Every day I'd work straight through until 10 p.m., taking an hour each for lunch and dinner, and then I'd catch the bus home in the dark. I'd shower and collapse into my bed to read for a few seconds in *Pigs Have Wings*, my latest Wodehouse novel, before falling asleep.

And that's how it went for seven straight days. I'd turn up at the Drug Fair at 8 a.m., an hour before the store opened, to prepare the potatoes for my demonstration. I'd restock the Veg-O-Matic display, piling the boxes high in an ergonomically conical construct of my own contrivance, and check out a register tray so that I could relieve cashiers who went on break.

If my schedule was exhausting, it also had its advantages. I slept like a stone, and the days flew by. At home, I didn't have a conversation with my mother, father, or sister that lasted more than 10 seconds. "Hi, how ya doing?" was as intimate as it got, which suited me. My father was asleep when I left in the morning and when I came in at night. I didn't have to listen to my mother and sister bicker. Only my brother Mike, with whom I shared a room, was around when I staggered in whacked out from twelve hours of working with the public. He'd fill me in on the day's drama with my sister, which made me glad I'd be headed back to college soon.

When the store closed at 9 p.m. on Christmas Eve, I used my humongous five percent employee discount to purchase gifts for the family—a cheap cotton bathrobe for my mother, which turned out to fit her like a circus tent, a simulated leather wallet for my father, a 45 of Donovan's "Catch the Wind" for my brother and the Beatles' *Help!* for my sister. I was headed out the door with my packages when the manager stopped me.

"You've done a good job," he said, a genuine smile on his pasty face. "And I'm hoping you'll consider coming back to work through New Year's Eve. You won't be selling Veg-O-Matics, but I need experienced help to run the registers and handle returns. I could use you for at least twelve hours a day."

Normally I would have responded with an emphatic "No," but fresh in my memory were the money problems I'd experienced during my first four months at college and the hours I spent in McEwen Dining Hall scraping greasy dishes and scrubbing pots. With my paltry allowance, there was no hope of establishing a relationship with any of the girls I found myself drooling over as they roamed the campus. It was essential I screw up my courage and get myself an on-campus date. I'd have to double with an upperclassman who had a car, and to make that happen, I needed enough money to cover my share of the gas.

"All right," I answered. "Can I get some overtime?"

"I'll give you all the overtime you want. You can work fourteen hours a day if you skip lunch and dinner."

"All right," I answered. "I'll be glad to help out."

So on December 27, I was standing behind a cash register refunding money for the Veg-O-Matics I'd sold the week before. "I'd like to get the money back for this thing," the customer would say, handing me the orange and black box. They occasionally offered excuses such as "I already have one of these" or "I have no use for this piece of junk," but what they wanted was cash. In almost every case the customer returning the Veg-O-Matic was not the person who'd bought it, so I didn't consider the returns a criticism of my performance. I handed them the money and stuck the boxes and signed receipts under the register. At the end of the day, I toted the returned Veg-O-Matics to the storeroom and piled them up in the same space they'd occupied when they were new.

To compound this irony, the manager handed me a hammer at closing time on my first post-Christmas day as a cashier and sent me to the stockroom to smash the Veg-O-Matics the store had taken back. "Just bash those veggie things into little bits and put them back in the boxes," he directed. "And while you're at it, smash up these toys that didn't get sold." The manager didn't explain why I needed to destroy so much perfectly good merchandise, and I didn't ask. But I laid into my new task with gusto, obliterating hundreds of Veg-O-Matics along with Chatty Cathy dolls, Etch A Sketches, tin airliners, space guns, trains, battery-powered James Bond Aston Martin cars, Rock 'Em Sock 'Em Robots, Easy-Bake Ovens, electric football games, G.I. Joes, and the occasional Barbie doll, perfectly good toys that might have gone to poor children who'd suffered a sad Christmas. But it was exhilarating work—and strangely gratifying—an anti-capitalistic binge that assuaged the guilt I'd suffered from selling plastic crap to poor people.

But the days were long, and there was no time to hang out with my friends. When I got off work at 9 p.m., I was too worn out to go to parties or ride around with high school buds. I'd catch the bus back to Eastport and fall into bed. The following morning, I'd get up and do it again.

On my last day of work, a Friday, the manager shook my hand. "You're a lifesaver," he said, pumping my weary arm. "If you need a job next Christmas, just let me know."

I smiled, gave him my college post office box number, and asked him to send my check there rather than to my home address.

"You should get it before the 10th," he said.

During the two and a half weeks I'd toiled at Drug Fair, my parents hardly noticed my absence. I was a shadow who flitted in and out at odd hours. And I wanted it that way. I didn't have to listen to them argue, which was their habitual method of communication during any holiday season when they were forced to remain in each other's company for more than five continuous minutes. And if my parents didn't realize the hours I was working, they'd have no idea how much money I was making. Had they an inkling of the cash I was likely to pocket, they would have given me that much less for tuition, room and board, and the endless hours I'd spent slaving at Drug Fair would have been for naught.

On the evening before my return to Elon, in honor of my having been invisible during the holiday season, my mother prepared lasagna, my favorite dish.

"You headed back tomorrow?" my father asked.

"First thing in the morning," I answered, "I'm going to catch the bus."

My mother looked puzzled. "It seems like you just got here," she said.

"I've been working the whole time."

"Good," she said. "How much money did you make?"

"I don't know. I haven't gotten paid yet—and the wage at Drug Fair isn't as much as it is at the Safeway. I'll let you know when the check arrives." I was lying, of course. I had no intention of telling anyone how much money I'd earned. It was nobody's business but my own.

# Eleven

I cupped my hands around my eyes and peered through the glass window in the brass door of my campus mailbox. Nothing. Still empty. I'd expected to receive my Drug Fair check no later than Monday, January 10, and when it didn't arrive, I slipped into a mild depression. Twice a day I'd check the mail, praying I'd glimpse an envelope resting slantwise in the box, and twice a day I walked away dejected.

It didn't take long for paranoia to set in. I lay awake at night imagining I'd been cheated out of my wages by the Drug Fair manager. What was to keep him from pocketing my earnings? He didn't give a damn about me. I was just another disposable nobody he ordered about, another meat robot. The little weasel hadn't even looked over the application I'd completed. Maybe he'd been scheming all along to steal the money I earned. I could hear him chuckling to himself: "That twerp worked his ass off and I'm keeping his money and there's nothing he can do about it!" Why had I believed it was possible to earn a few bucks working for a screen-door operation like Drug Fair?

I remained in a foul mood until January 15, when the check miraculously appeared in my mailbox. I spun the combination mechanism to the correct letters, yanked open the brass door, and tore into the envelope. I'd earned $196.46 after taxes, a veritable fortune! Dividing by the number of months in the spring semester, I'd more than doubled my disposable income. No more schmoozing my parents. No more pinching pennies. I could buy my books for the spring term and still have at least $160 left, enough to have myself a high ole time. I marched into the bookstore, bought the books I lacked, and stuffed the wad of bills into my pocket. Then I quick-timed it to McEwen and quit my pot-scrubbing job. I told the one-armed cafeteria manager that I needed to focus on my studies, which wasn't a lie, and he shook my right hand with his left and thanked me for being dependable.

With my surplus funds safely stashed in the breast pocket of my Harris Tweed sports jacket tucked in the back of my closet, I should have spent the remaining two weeks of the semester in a state of bliss. Instead, I began to anguish over my impending finals. Although I'd regularly attended class and taken careful notes when there weren't seductive females lounging about on the lawn outside the classroom windows, I was wracked with insecurities. If I failed my exams there was a good chance I'd receive Fs in my courses, even though I'd maintained mostly B averages during the semester. I had to keep telling myself that I had a measure of control over the grades I'd earn on exams. All I had to do was put in some study time, and I knew how to do that.

What I *wasn't* going to do was pull "all-nighters," which seemed to be the plan that most of my friends had adopted. What was the point of staying up for twenty-four hours pretending to study and going to the exam in a stupor? I spent my time reviewing my class notes—except in English, where I'd been unable to discern any consistent theme, other than Reed's adamant opposition to the war and his fixation on student incompetence.

The other guys on second Smith had their own methods for coping with finals. A few sad souls made no preparations whatsoever, safe in the knowledge that their college careers were over no matter what grades they received on their exams. A casual acquaintance explained his rationale for *not* preparing for finals. "I used to study and get an F," he said, "and then I'd feel like a real asshole. Now I don't study at all, and when I get an F, I'm fine with it. I say to myself, 'Hey, you didn't study a lick for that exam. So what do you expect?'" A few of the more serious students organized study groups for religion, business math, western civ, etc., and a couple of lost souls procured black beauties, a readily available amphetamine, to help them stay awake all night in hopes of cramming into a few hours what they'd failed to absorb in four months.

And there were, of course, the clowns who were into cheating, which occurs at all colleges and universities. One maniac—he'd come to Elon hoping to play basketball but had gotten cut early in the season—spent days coming up with new and ingenious methods for beating the system. To prepare for his biology exam, he scratched the thirty-five phyla of the kingdom Animalia onto the flat surfaces of a red heptagon pencil, and did the same with the kingdom Plantae on a green pencil. He cut tiny slivers of paper with a razor blade and printed possible answers to his economics final in various colored inks. On the first day of exams, he'd concealed so many cheat sheets on his person that he had to wear a shirt with double pockets and a cardigan sweater with two large pouches in the front. In one of the pouches he secreted a "master crib sheet," which directed him to the other crib sheets hidden on his person—"meiosis, right shirt pocket and homeostasis, left sweater pocket"—all written in microscopic letters.

I figured the process of preparing to cheat took longer and required more effort than studying the subject matter. Moreover,

Elon had an honor code. We were required to write and sign a pledge at the bottom of each exam—"I have neither given nor received assistance on this test nor have I seen anyone doing so." To avoid violating the pledge, I employed a lawyer's dodge: I hadn't actually *seen* my friend cheat, so I wasn't guilty of anything. A student caught cheating would be dragged before an honor court to plead his case. If he was found guilty, he was kicked out of college and his draft board was notified. Next stop: Southeast Asia.

Most of my finals were what I'd expected, straightforward short essay, multiple choice, and matching, the kind of exams professors can grade quickly (students aren't the only people in academe who are lazy), and by January 22, I'd taken all my finals except English, which was scheduled for January 26 at 10 a.m. Since there was no possible way to study for Reed's exam, I had the weekend free.

• • •

On Saturday afternoon, Tindall and I hitched into Burlington and hung out for a couple of hours at the B&B Smoke Shop. Then we hoofed it over to Zack's for chili and slaw hot dogs and fries, and strolled uptown to a pawnshop, where we examined musical instruments—guitars, banjos, mandolins, etc.—stuff we couldn't begin to afford. Midafternoon we decided to knock back a few more brews, so we cut through the gift department of Sellars Department Store and walked up the cold concrete sidewalk on Lexington and South Spring streets to the Sportsmen Bar. We'd never frequented the Sportsmen, which catered to local millworkers, and we must have appeared sadly out of place with our longish hair and Yankee clothes. A couple of regulars playing table shuffleboard in a dimly lit corner stared at us as we wandered in, and the bartender gave us the once over before asking, "What'll you boys have?"

While drinking my 25-cent drafts, I noticed cartons of cigarettes stacked on a counter behind the bar. The packaging was like none I'd ever seen, retro before retro was an adjective, evocative of late nineteenth-century art, the kind of kitschy stuff I liked.

"How much for a pack of those cigarettes?" I asked the bartender.

"Which ones?"

"The ones with the baseball players on the front."

"Home Run cigarettes are 15 cents a pack."

"I'll take three packs," I said, digging a fistful of change out of my pocket. "How much are the others?" I added, pointing to a stack of smokes in white and blue wrappers.

"The Piedmonts are the same price."

"Give me three packs of those, too."

The bartender slid the six packs of cigarettes across the bar. I counted out the correct change and pushed it in his direction.

"They ain't puttin' baseball cards in them Piedmonts no more," he grumbled as he rang up the sale.

"That's all right," I said, holding up the Home Runs. "What do you know about these cigarettes? Where do they come from?"

"At the end of each day when they sweep up the floor at the cigarette factory," the bartender explained, "they use the crud and loose tobacco to make Home Runs."

I didn't smoke, and I had no plans to start. But I was pleased with my purchase. "Look at these," I said to Tindall. "Are they cool enough?"

He examined the Home Runs in their drab green and beige packaging. Printed in muted tones on the front of each pack were a catcher and a batter in turn-of-the-century baseball garb. They were waiting for an invisible pitcher to send the ball.

"What are you going to do with those things?" Tindall asked.

"You don't smoke."

"I don't know," I said, shrugging my shoulders. "They're cool. That's enough."

On Monday I did my best to prepare for Reed's final exam. I outlined an essay that made a strong case for withdrawing our troops from Vietnam, and then I sat staring at a blank sheet of paper wondering what other possible essay topics Reed might spring on us. There was an outside chance he'd concoct a syntactical Hydra-headed essay question that combined his concerns about the war in Vietnam with Edith Hamilton's *Mythology*, the text we never opened during the course, so I wrote out a possible topic in my notebook: "Compare and contrast Odysseus and Aeneas and their differing concepts of heroism, using contemporary examples to illustrate how governments manipulate their citizens to display heroism in battle and to encourage genocide." I could probably bluff my way through the opinion part of such an essay, but I'd be lost if I had to write something intelligent about Odysseus and Aeneas. After a few hours of torment, I tossed my fortunes to the wind and crawled into the sack.

I couldn't fall asleep. As I tossed and turned in the darkness, worries began to eat away at the edges of my consciousness. The war in Vietnam and damn draft, both of which were growing more ominous with each passing week, kept gnawing at me. The previous Wednesday evening I'd stopped by the library to read the latest *Time* and *Newsweek*, and the news from Southeast Asia was nothing but bad. The number of Americans killed in action was rising, and I'd read that the draft boards were yanking students out of the classroom. I lay in bed imagining a nefarious bureaucrat sitting in a dimly lit office in the Selective Service Building (if there was such a place) perusing my file (if I had a file) and contriving ways in which he or she might ruin my life—or worse, end it. I spent the night worrying myself into a state of acute consternation.

• • •

I turned up for Reed's exam at the appointed time, a hefty breakfast of eggs, sausage and toast gurgling in the pit of my stomach, a pack of Home Run cigarettes stuffed in my shirt pocket for luck and took my regular seat. Reed was, as usual, fifteen minutes late. He strutted into the classroom, brushed his shellacked cowlick out of his eyes, pushed up a window sash and flipped his Lucky Strike into the January morning. As he stared pensively into the horizon over Lebanon Avenue, I surveyed my fellow sufferers. Of the twenty students who were in the class on the first day, four of us remained.

Reed had instructed us to bring a pen and ten sheets of blank paper to the exam. "If you can't write an essay in ten pages, you can't write an essay," he'd said during the last class period. I sat with my BIC poised, my ears pricked forward, my heart thumping.

"All right," Reed said. "Write an essay in which you discuss why we shouldn't be in Vietnam." And he sat down at his desk and stared at us.

That was it? I waited for Reed to give us the second part of the essay topic, but there was only silence. I was dumbfounded. I'd suffered not a little anguish contriving possible esoteric essay questions, and Reed had apparently rattled off whatever happened to pop into his head as he flipped his cigarette out the window. He hadn't even bothered to write the topic on the chalkboard. When Reed stepped into the hall, I began to scribble, slowly at first but picking up speed with each sentence. After an hour and a half, I decided to take a break.

I'm not a big believer in destiny. Everything is an accident, the product of a trillion other accidents, but if the hand of providence ever touched me, it was at that instant. I stepped into the hall, and there was Tully Reed staring me full in the face. Every cell in my body underwent an instantaneous transformation. I hadn't expected to find him propped against the wall. We both stood dead still. Then he wadded up an empty Lucky Strike package and dropped it in a trash can he'd been using as an ashtray. He was out of cigarettes.

I was at a complete loss about what I should say or do. And that's when I remembered the Home Runs in my shirt pocket, which I'd intended to use as an excuse for taking a break during the exam. Reed was a chain smoker; he couldn't refuse a poor nicotine-addicted student a drag or two on a cigarette. And now Reed was jonesing for a smoke, and I had an unopened pack at my fingertips. I wasn't a brownnoser by nature—kowtowing was flat-out against the rules—but I'd been granted a rare opportunity.

"Would you like a cigarette, Professor Reed?" I asked.

He stared at me, balancing pride against addiction. "Sure," he said.

I snatched the pack of unopened Home Runs out of my shirt pocket, pulled the red tab that removed the cellophane, unfolded the foil, tapped a single cigarette halfway out and held out the package. Reed's eyes bulged.

"Home Run cigarettes!" he exclaimed. "My great uncle used to smoke Home Run cigarettes! I haven't seen a pack of those in thirty years!"

"Here," I said, in a steady voice. "Keep the pack." I was acting on instinct, but I was confident that I'd made the slickest move of my life. I was suave and sophisticated and absolutely sure of myself. I'd done everything but light the cigarette à la Paul Henreid and pass it over.

He took the pack in his hand and examined the illustration

of the ballplayers. "Thirty years," he said again, shaking his head. He carefully removed the cigarette, put it between his lips, and lit it with his Zippo. He inhaled deeply and smiled, smoke snorting from his nostrils. "Not bad," he said, and took a second deeper drag. "Where on earth did you get these?"

"They sell them at the Sportsmen Bar."

"Really?"

"Next time I'm in Burlington, I can get you as many packs as you'd like." Hell, I would have bought him fifty cartons of Home Runs if it would secure an A for me in freshman English.

"No, no. This is fine," he answered, no doubt pleased with my offering.

"What's your name?" he asked.

I'd been sitting in his class for an entire semester, more than four months, and he had no idea who I was.

I said my name slowly.

"You're in this comp class?"

"Yes, sir."

He knitted his brow. "Didn't you bring me one of your essays to go over?"

"Yes, sir."

"I remember that. Pretty good essay."

A pretty good essay! Great God Almighty, I was saved! I half expected to ascend then and there unto the left hand of God the Father Almighty. Hardly trusting my luck and feeling a trifle smug, I said, "Well, I'd better get back to work. I've got an exam to complete."

He smiled and nodded, a cloud of acrid smoke encircling his smiling face. I hurried back into the classroom to finish my essay on why America had no business in Vietnam.

As I reviewed the gibberish I'd scribbled, I was bathed in the exquisite euphoria occasioned by Reed's unabashed approval. He'd acknowledged that I'd written a "pretty good essay." I'd made a positive, lasting impression on the scourge of the English Department. I might pass the class after all! I could visualize Reed looking over the English comp exams and scratching a big red F on each one until he happened upon my handiwork. "Ah, yes," he would say to himself, "this is the fine fellow who gave me the pack of Home Run cigarettes. What a great student—A+."

I was in a state of jubilation for the remainder of the day, and that night, Gene Matthews and I hitched to the Tap Room, where I drank copious amounts of beer to celebrate my good fortune. Maybe I'd make the dean's list after all.

"I can't believe it," I said to Gene. "I handed Reed the pack of Home Runs, and he said that I had written a pretty good essay!"

As Gene and I were leaving the Tap Room, our coat collars buttoned against the January cold, he asked, "You going home for break?"

"Naw," I said. "I don't think so."

Why waste money on a long and tedious bus ride? I'd made the trip three times in the last four months, and I was sick of watching the Virginia countryside slide by like the setting in an Erskine Caldwell novel. With autumn behind us, the trees were stark and gray, and the road was lined with shabby gas stations and truck-stop diners.

"I'll stay over and maybe do some studying. I'm on a roll."

# Twelve

I awakened early on Thursday, January 27, and stared bleary-eyed out my dorm window. The college was blanketed with at least six inches of new snow—and it was still falling, drifting over the campus wall and clinging in heavy knots to the limbs of oaks and sycamores. What had been Haggard Avenue was now a trackless expanse of white.

I'd planned on staying over during semester break to get ahead in my coursework, but the sight of new snow stirred in me an irrational desire to get back to Annapolis. The day before, I'd imagined myself alone on second Smith. No music. No talk. Solitude. Brinkley had headed to Virginia the previous Friday, and I had the room all to myself. Now I hated the idea of being confined to the dorm for the next five days with nothing to do but read *The Great Gatsby*, which was required of all second-semester freshmen. I staggered to the door and stared down the cold, dark hallway. I'd been alone for only five minutes, and already the absence of my friends was vaguely disturbing.

I'd written down the number of a junior in Carolina Hall who'd been recruiting riders for a trip to Baltimore, so I phoned him and asked if he still planned on driving north. "I'm not gonna play dodgem cars with a bunch of dumbass Southerners who don't know how to drive in this mess," he said.

I was trapped.

The snow continued to fall all morning, and shortly before noon I decided to set out on my own. I donned my car coat and scarf, stuffed two $20 bills in my pants pocket, grabbed my copy of *Gatsby* and galumphed through waist-deep drifts to Williamson Avenue, where I caught a ride in a pickup truck slipping and sliding out to I-85. A UNC student in a four-wheel drive Willys panel wagon gave me a lift to Washington Street in Greensboro, where the old Southern Railway depot rose out of the whiteness, its Ionic columns supporting a pedimented portico, the building's interior lights winking through the storm. I hurried inside and slapped down a $20 bill for a ticket north on the Peach Queen.

By the mid-'60s, the railroads had fallen on hard times, but the Greensboro depot was still inspiring with its vaulted ceiling and bowl-shaded alabaster chandeliers. Above the doors to the platform, a large color map of the Southern Railways System dominated the waiting room. On the far side of the lobby, ranks of back-to-back benches provided seating for forty to fifty determined travelers.

"You're going to have a long wait," the ticket agent informed me. "Every college kid in the South is traveling in this snowstorm, and the Peach Queen is running late."

I placed a collect call to my mother and told her I'd be arriving in DC in the early morning hours.

"Why don't you stay there?" she asked. "It's going to snow here, too."

"I don't know," I answered. "I feel like coming home. Anyway, I'm already at the train station and I've paid for my ticket. I can't get back to Elon in this weather."

"I'll have your father meet you," she said, sounding mildly annoyed.

I occupied a corner seat on one of the benches and began reading *Gatsby*: "In my younger and more vulnerable years . . ." I wanted to like the novel, but I found it tough going. I didn't know anyone like Nick Carraway or Tom and Daisy Buchanan. My family didn't drive a swanky, chrome-plated automobile or live in a mansion with a swimming pool, but I soldiered on into chapter seven before I grew discouraged and my attention waned. When a Guilford College junior produced a deck of cards and asked if I'd like to play a few hands of penny ante poker, I obliged.

As the evening wore on and the snow continued to fall, a group of five or six of us dealt hands and traded stories about the trials and tribulations of college life. It wasn't long before an esprit developed among those of us trapped in the drafty old station, and the conversation shifted to the Vietnam War. We were of one mind: It was a stupid waste of life in a place none of us cared about. "I'm not going to go ten thousand miles to kill people who haven't done a thing to me," the Guilford College student said. "Why are we fighting to hold on to a scrap of land of no value to us? The Communists aren't going to climb into boats and storm ashore in New York City."

"I won't be returning after the break," a Greensboro College sophomore announced. "They changed my draft status to 1-A. I'm going for a physical in February—but I plan on enlisting before that, maybe try to get in the Coast Guard or something."

"Just flunk the physical," someone advised.

"How do I do that?" the sophomore asked.

"Put a penny under your tongue. It'll send your blood pressure sky high."

What followed was a series of suggestions on how to fail the draft physical, which included wearing women's undergarments, feigning insanity, and hacking off your trigger finger.

"Apply for conscientious objector status," a sophomore from Guilford College, a Quaker school, suggested, "and if that doesn't work, go to Canada."

A kid from High Point College who had failed his physical because of a blood pressure reading of 200/110, claimed that his hypertension was his "body protecting itself," and went on to spin a lengthy yarn about a college football player who'd taken the physical with him. "He was on a scholarship at the University of Pennsylvania and was in pretty good shape, but when he completed the form listing the diseases he'd had, he checked everything— arthritis, heart disease, stroke, brain tumor, colon cancer, diabetes, and epilepsy. He told the sergeant that he had bad knees and a fractured pelvis. And when they put earphones on him and shut him in that glass booth they use for the hearing test, he pretended he couldn't hear anything. They turned the tone up so loud we could hear it outside the booth, and he sat there with this stupid grin on his face. If he wasn't deaf before the test, he was after. Last time I saw him he was telling the sergeant that he was a homosexual and wanted to speak to a shrink."

"Did it work?" the guy from Greensboro College asked.

"I never saw him again."

I decided to give *Gatsby* another try and eased out of the card game, having broken even. Above the chatter, I could hear music emanating from a tinny, high-pitched transistor radio in a far corner of the room where three or four college-age couples were Shagging. I found a seat near the music and watched the dancers, focusing on a handsome couple who moved with the easy grace of professionals. They had taken off their snowshoes, and slipped into their Nettletons and Pappagallos, and their feet glided effortlessly across the granite floor. The boy's blond hair was cut in an obligatory pageboy that ruffled faintly as he guided his partner through twirls and precise shuffles, their bodies swaying to and fro, the balls of their feet barely touching the floor. The girl had a thin, sweet face and shiny auburn air that eddied and undulated as she followed her partner's precise lead. So intent were they on their dancing that their faces were devoid of expression, except for the boy's lips moving silently as he counted time—one-and-two, three-and-four, five-six—each syllable corresponding to a step, as Gene Matthews had shown me after my disastrous effort to dance at freshman orientation.

"Would you like to dance?" someone asked.

I looked into the face of a woman with a wide toothy smile, her blond hair pulled back in a ponytail. She wasn't the most desirable woman in the room—a little bulky in the hips and shoulders and probably taller than I was—but she was the first eligible female who had spoken to me voluntarily in the last six months. I was dumbstruck.

"It'll be a while before the train gets here," she added.

I couldn't come up with an appropriate response. A female hadn't asked me to dance since I had attempted to learn the box step in fourth-grade physical education. I managed only a throaty grumble in response.

"Come on," she said. "You haven't got anything else to do but read that boring book."

I responded with the truth: "I don't know how to dance like that."

"Well, I'll show you how," she said and took my hand.

I put *Gatsby* aside and stepped onto the improvised dance floor, taking a flatfooted stance that left me staring up into the woman's jade-green eyes. The radio DJ announced a new single by

Chris Montez, "The More I See You," a lazy middle-of-the-road tune with multiple hand claps supplying the backbeat, perfect for dancing the Shag. The other couples stepped off smoothly. I stood there with my mouth agape.

"All right," she said. "Feel the rhythm and begin to sway back and forth like this." She moved her outsized shoulders and hips in unison. "You're going to move back and forth, back and forth, and alternate your feet. Imagine you're a pendulum."

I did as directed, shuffling forward and back, doing my best to stay in step with her as she skimmed the floor.

"You don't want to bounce when you're dancing the Shag," she said. "It needs to be fluid."

I gave the step an equally awkward second try.

"That's a little better," she said, "but stay on the balls of your feet, like this." She slid up and back on her tiptoes in perfect time to the music. I stumbled along as best I could, a half beat behind her. Unfortunately, there was no connection between my befuddled cerebellum and my feet. Chris Montez saved me by limiting his recording time to a little more than two minutes, and the song was over before I became the subject of widespread ridicule.

"I should practice this step some more, maybe on my own," I said, and returned to my seat. My former dance partner found a willing and able victim, one more her size, on a bench a few feet away and led him onto the dance floor, where they moved as if they'd been dancing together since birth.

• • •

The conductor called "All aboard!" at about 11 p.m., and my fellow refugees and I climbed onto an olive-drab heavyweight prewar passenger car that had been added to the train to accommodate the increase in ridership. I lucked into a window seat vacated by a passenger who was detraining. The heat wasn't working properly and the lighting was poor, but I continued reading *Gatsby* as we lurched out of Greensboro and rocked into the countryside. By the time we'd left Danville, Fitzgerald was waxing poetic:

> *When we pulled out into the winter night and the real snow, our snow, began to stretch out beside us and twinkle against the windows, and the dim lights of small Wisconsin stations moved by, a sharp wild brace came suddenly into the air. We drew in deep breaths of it as we walked back from dinner through the cold vestibules, unutterably aware of our identity with this country for one strange hour, before we melted indistinguishably into it again.*

I closed *Gatsby*, rubbed a circle in the frosty filigreed window glass, and watched as the lights of anonymous Virginia towns swirled by in the snowy darkness. Perhaps Fitzgerald was correct: the future was already gone, lost in the vast obscurity where *"the dark fields of the republic rolled on under the night."*

About 9:30 a.m., the Peach Queen shrieked to a halt in DC's Union Station. I stared out the grimy window and spotted my father, wrapped to his ears in a heavy wool overcoat and scarf, waiting on the platform. The first semester of my freshman year was gone.

February-August 1966

# Thirteen

Consternation was rampant on the second floor of McEwen Dining Hall where freshmen were packed cheek to jowl to register for spring semester courses. Teeth gnashing, fists pounding, cussing, abject desperation reigned. It was mayhem.

It was 2:45 p.m., and I'd been standing in line since 8:30 a.m., trying to nail down a few courses for the spring semester. Classes that had closed out because of maximum enrollment were written on a chalkboard at the far end of the room. If a course I'd tentatively signed up for appeared on the board, I had to get back in line to consult with Dr. Stokes, who would then suggest an alternate class that would soon enough appear on the list of closed courses. When that happened, I had to begin again, rearranging my schedule. Then I had to get back in line to have Dr. Stokes approve those changes. It was infuriating. A student could conceivably stand in line for the remainder of his natural life. I wanted to climb up on one of the registration tables and scream, "Will somebody please fix this mess?"

I was further aggravated by the rumor that registration was rigged. The mimeographed schedule didn't identify which professor taught what course, but the inside skinny was that football and basketball players had a list of the easy professors that taught the difficult classes, and they'd gobbled up the easy courses early on. The rest of us were left to blindly stumble around the registration process and hope for the best. I needed three more hours in English, and I sure as hell didn't relish struggling through another semester with Tully Reed.

"Is there another English course I could sign up for?" I asked Dr. Stokes. "You know, maybe a creative writing course or something like that?"

I was smug enough to believe I could wheedle my way into a creative writing class. I might even make a decent grade if the professor was competent.

"We offer creative writing but not during the spring semester," Dr. Stokes said. "Sign up for the course next fall."

"Who teaches it?" I asked.

"Manly Wellman," Dr. Stokes said. "He's got an office on the third floor of the Carlton Building. He's probably on campus today; he usually comes in during registration to discuss grades with his fall semester students. If you're interested, go see him. He might reserve a place for you in the fall semester."

"There must be an English Comp I can sign up for," I said.

"Look here," Dr. Stokes said, running his index finger down the schedule. "I can put you in a 1 o'clock Monday, Wednesday, Friday English 112."

"Ok, I'll take that," I said. "I hope it stays open until my schedule is entered. This is the fifth time I've had to change everything."

"I know it's a mess," Dr. Stokes said, "but we'll get it done. Be patient. It's one of those little inconveniences we encounter in life."

"Is this the way life is going to be?" I asked, half kidding.

"Pretty much," Dr. Stokes replied, giving it to me straight.

To compound my frustration, semester break had been a

disaster. While at home, I'd phoned a few old high school girlfriends to arrange a date, but most of them were going steady with midshipmen. "Ah, come on," I begged an old flame who'd taken a job as a secretary with Nationwide. "We'll go to a movie or something. No big deal...." After ten minutes of enduring my begging, she grew as frustrated as I was and hung up. Instead of hitting one of the local dance clubs with a date, I had to labor away my four days at home helping my father staple up an acoustic tile ceiling in the rec room. To make matters worse, my grades arrived on Saturday, January 29, and I hadn't made the dean's list. Most distressingly, Reed had given me a C- in English 111, despite my gift of Home Run cigarettes and probably the best essay he'd received all semester. I'd fallen short of an overall B average.

On the last day of January, I endured an excruciating twelve-hour bus ride from DC to Burlington—and I had to pay for the ticket myself! When I asked my father to help me out with a couple of extra bucks, he gave me the old spiel, "You'll have to wait until I deposit your allowance into your checking account. You need to budget your money more wisely."

"Tomorrow's the first of the month," I said. "What's a few hours?"

"You'll have to wait until tomorrow. That's the way it is."

"I was hoping maybe you could shovel a little more coal into the boiler," I quipped, alluding to the letter in which he characterized himself as a stoker in the ship's engine room.

"What the hell are you talking about?" he asked. "You made money over the holidays. What happened to it?"

I shrugged.

• • •

It was 3:30 p.m. before I'd secured the courses I needed. As I walked by the entrance to Carlton, I paused to consider looking up this Wellman guy. Why not? I had an hour and a half before dinner and nothing to do during the interval. I could talk with him for a couple of minutes and get myself set up for his creative writing course in the fall. So I climbed the stairs to the third floor of Carlton and found the hallway dark except for a rectangle of light projecting from an open doorway. The clack-clack of a manual typewriter echoed as I approached the office, where I paused again before looking inside. Did I want to waste my time chewing the fat with some old fuddy-duddy? But I was already there, so I stuck my head into the tiny office and said, "Excuse me."

An elderly man sat at an oak desk, bare except for a black portable Royal typewriter. The 8x8 room lacked bookshelves, filing cabinets, and wall art. An old leather briefcase was angled against the desk. Tapping on the typewriter was Manly Wade Wellman.

Wellman was barrel-chested and wide-shouldered, his graying hair combed back from his broad forehead. His round, open face was accentuated with heavy eyebrows and a prominent nose below which was cultivated a tweedy, slightly skewed Clark Gable mustache. What was immediately appreciable was the peculiar way in which his eyes reflected light. The very tops of his dark irises flickered, suggesting an inner illumination. He was dressed neatly in a frayed sports jacket that matched his mustache. A bulky glasses case was stuffed in the pocket of his blue shirt. A bolo tie clinched by a silver and turquoise medallion hung loose around his neck. He was smoking a cigarillo clutched in his right hand, the ring and little finger of which were stunted.

"Come in, come in," he said in a booming voice.

I tentatively ventured into the office. "Are you Professor Wellman?" I asked.

"I am," he said.

I introduced myself and told him I was interested in signing up for his creative writing class in the fall.

"Have a seat," he said. "Let's chat."

And that's what we did, for about an hour. Wellman began by asking what my major was. I said I hadn't decided for sure but was leaning toward sociology—which wasn't true. I'd made no decision about a major but felt I should answer the question. Sociology was the first major that popped into my head.

"There's no such thing as sociology," he replied, emphatically. "Don't waste your time. You'll want to major in something that exists."

If Wellman was insistent, he was also endearing. I was immediately convinced that this guy had a sincere interest in who I was and what I thought. He wanted to know about my latest writing project as if it were of immense concern to the literary community. "What are you working on?" he asked.

I'd written only one crummy short story and a sappy poem in high school. "Gosh, I don't know," I said.

"What is your favorite book of fiction?" he asked, leaning forward and tapping the ash off his cigarillo onto the floor.

If I'd told the truth, I would have said P.G. Wodehouse or I might have mentioned the author of *Last Exit to Brooklyn*, if I could have remembered his name, but I didn't want Wellman to believe I was a reader of fluffy or pornographic fiction, so I dropped Bruce Catton's name instead, even though I knew that Catton wrote nonfiction. "I liked *A Stillness at Appomattox*."

"I've written a few Civil War books myself," he boasted. "Any other favorites?"

"I've read Hemingway's *A Farewell to Arms*, and I like Robert Frost's poems." I hadn't read much of Frost, only the verse that appeared in the high school literature texts of the time—"Stopping by Woods on a Snowy Evening," "Mending Wall," and "The Road Not Taken"—but I felt compelled to mention a writer who wielded intellectual oomph.

Wellman grunted. "We don't write poetry in my class. Have you read Thomas Wolfe?"

"I've heard of him," I said, "but I've never read anything he's written."

"Wolfe is the greatest writer North Carolina ever produced. You need to read him before you take my class. That's the best advice I can give you—read Thomas Wolfe." He paused. "You know that Thomas Wolfe used to ride the train from Asheville to Chapel Hill and it would stop here, and Wolfe and his friends would stick their head out of the windows and yell, 'Elon, Elon, girls, girls, girls!'"

I stared, not knowing what my response should be.

"And you ought to read James Joyce too," he continued. "Begin with *Dubliners* and work your way through *Ulysses*. Those are two books every writer should read. And read Twain's *Huck Finn*, if you haven't already."

I wasn't even signed up for this guy's class and he was giving me reading assignments.

"I'll get copies and read them this semester," I promised, knowing that I probably wouldn't.

"There'd be no contemporary American writers," he continued, "not in the sense that we know them, without Twain. Let me tell you a story about him." He leaned gently forward again, indicating that he was about to share a confidence. "When my father was a boy, my grandfather took him to hear a lecture by Twain. They found seats in the front of the lecture hall, and when Twain walked out on the stage in a white suit and puffing a cigar, he withdrew a folded sheet of paper from his inside coat pocket and stared at the audience. 'I've written a poem, and I'd like to read it for you,' Twain said. And the audience laughed. Twain was a humorist, and they thought he was joking. But he stared at them and said, 'Don't laugh. This is a serious poem.' And they laughed again. So Twain crumpled up the paper and tossed it on the stage. When he'd finished his lecture, he walked off, leaving the discarded poem behind. My father, who was eight or nine at the time, wanted to reach out and grab it, but his father led him from the room. Before leaving the building, he looked back and saw a janitor sweeping the stage. Twain's poem went into a trash can."

No doubt Wellman intended some analogous revelation, but I was distracted by the sensuously affective images he'd employed to embellish his story: that long-ago evening when the romantic possibility of a white-haired, cigar-puffing Twain existed in America, the ingenuously irreverent audience, the small boy longing to rescue the Great Lost American Poem. It was all there, spun forth in Wellman's raspy baritone, rising and falling with modulations of passion, poignancy, and a trace of regret. Upon arriving at the anecdote's climax, his tone dropped an octave below my ability to comprehend. I leaned forward as his voice rose to a crescendo.

"If only my father had reached out and grabbed that poem when he had the chance!" he roared, his stunted right hand darting across the desktop.

Startled, I sat upright in my chair. And that's when I realized that Manly Wade Wellman was speaking in the voice in which he wrote—or more precisely, wrote as he was speaking. If the story was a metaphor, he didn't belabor the obvious, and perhaps that was also part of the lesson: A good story speaks for itself.

"When you're ready to take creative writing, drop me a note and I'll give you permission," he said. "I only accept eight students in the class." We chatted for a few more minutes, but I sensed

Wellman had said all he had to say to me. I excused myself and walked back down the dark hallway. I could hear the clacking of his portable typewriter and smell the acrid cigarillo smoke, and I knew that I'd sign up for creative writing as soon as I could get around to it, which, unfortunately, would be another two years.

• • •

The following day I hurried to the library and checked out *Look Homeward, Angel*. Since I'd already read *The Great Gatsby*, I decided to read a few of Fitzgerald's short stories, so I grabbed a copy of *Taps at Reveille*. While there, I flipped through *Books in Print* until I got to "Wellman." My God! There were about fifty listings for Manly Wade Wellman. Maybe he knew something about what he was teaching. He'd written a shelf full of books. Still, I was skeptical, possessed of the terrible notion that afflicts most college students: If this guy is any good, why would he be interested in teaching me?

If Wellman had inspired me, Thomas Wolfe kicked my butt. I read forty pages of *Look Homeward, Angel* that evening. And like many impressionable readers, I was smitten with his prose style—all those adjectives and adverbs strung together in long poetic passages that explored the relationship of the past to the present.

With Wolfe's prose fresh in my brain, I sat down and wrote in longhand what I thought might be the beginning or the end of my first novel:

"Sliding his fingers nervously through his hair, he placed the lamp on the desk and seated himself in the ancient rocker. He watched the woman sleep. Her light brown hair lay in a tangled web on the pillow and he saw, as he had seen so many times before, the gentle quiet etching of the face and the slightly parted lips of sleep, and then, slowly, something rare welled deep within his brain—a tender lonely feeling that came at times such as this—and it thrust him backward into remembrance, a deep and fierce remembrance of those lost years—years by whose fated whim he came to sit now, a tortured man, and he stared like a stranger at the only person he had ever truly known."

 I read the narrative passage a couple of times and was confident it was nothing less than genius, at least as good as what Wolfe had written—maybe better—and I was determined to send Manly Wade Wellman a copy at my first opportunity. Probably he'd put me in touch with a publisher, and my career as a writer would take off from there. I folded the pages I'd written and stuffed them in my notebook. That night, I put my head on my pillow, convinced that I was bound to be a major American writer.

 When I awakened the next morning, I reread my handiwork and was amazed how overnight my masterpiece had become tedious and pretentious. I wasn't sure what it was about or where it was going, but I recognized the distinctive rhythms of Thomas Wolfe's prose style. I was a plagiarist.

 I spent the remainder of the day reviewing my conversation with the charismatic writer I'd found pecking away at his typewriter on the third floor of Carlton. I couldn't help but wonder how my freshman comp class might have been more rewarding had my professor been Manly Wellman. I certainly wouldn't have been fearful of attending class, and I would have listened carefully to his every word. He was undeniably compelling—and inspiring! There are professors who can change your life for the better, and forever, and I sensed in my bones that Manly Wade Wellman was one of those miraculous human beings.

# Fourteen

Hunched over the steering wheel of a borrowed Renault Dauphine on a frigid Saturday night in early February, I searched the scattered outskirts of Greensboro for the Castaways, the beach music club that was all the snazz with college kids in the Triad. As I turned off East Bessemer Avenue onto Arnold Street, my date, her teeth chattering and her London Fog overcoat buttoned to her chin, pressed her index finger to the icy windshield and blurted, "That's it!"

"That's the Castaways?" I asked.

We'd already wound our way through a mile of repurposed World War II-era warehouses, and it appeared to me that we'd happened onto another block of similar structures. But my date was correct—an outsized blue sign atop the centermost building proclaimed in cursive: *The Castaways*.

It wasn't what I'd expected of the premier dance club in the Piedmont. Where were the flashing colored lights beckoning us to the entrance? Why was there no queue of college kids waiting anxiously to guzzle cold Blue Ribbon and dance to live music? The barren, trash-strewn street was empty except for thirty or forty cars parked haphazardly at the curb and in an adjoining gravel parking lot. The building was a one-story masonry warehouse with a steel door slammed into a beige Perma-Stone façade.

• • •

During my first semester at Elon, the Castaways was the destination of choice for any guy with a date and transportation, which excluded freshmen such as myself, who were at the bottom of the pecking order when it came to procuring female companionship and weren't allowed to keep cars on campus. I'd heard the club advertised the previous September on WBAG, Burlington's top-40 radio station, when the Toys, a female trio who'd had a hit single with "A Lover's Concerto," a cloying love lyric set to Bach's "Minuet in G major," were scheduled to perform. I asked Townie about the Castaways, and he explained that it catered to college kids—whites only—and featured local bands, also white, and the occasional Motown, Atlantic, Stax or other black R&B acts performing popular music for dancing the Shag. "If you're going to the Castaways," Townie cautioned, "you better know how to dance right."

Despite the sinister neighborhood—Arnold Street was a likely location for a mugging—a wave of anticipation surged through me as I guided the Renault into the parking lot. Sitting beside me, close enough to feel the warmth of her breath and detect the faint presence of her perfume, sat my first college date. Tindall, who was handy with nicknames, had dubbed her "Blondie," not after the beautiful, ditsy wife of Dagwood Bumstead in the funny papers but because she was so exquisitely fair that we regarded her as unapproachable. Occasionally, one of the second Smith gang would brush by her in a hallway. "I passed Blondie today on my way to Business Math," he'd report dutifully. "You did?" someone would ask. "How'd she look?" The answer was "scrumptious" or "gorgeous," or "stunning." She was never the subject of tactless vulgarities or the unflattering adjectives employed to describe the less inspiring campus girls.

Although attractive when measured by the conformist ideals of the day, I'd observed that she wasn't without imperfections—her gait was a touch wonky, and she tended to laugh too brashly when she was the center of a gaggle of her dorm friends—but she was as close to flawless as any girl on campus. Her porcelain, perfectly proportioned face was framed by iridescent, shoulder-length blond hair, and she stared out at the world through two large ethereal blue eyes. Her casual smile, which she occasionally crinkled into a tiny moue, was enigmatic and suggested a hint of unpredictability. But what made her exceptional, what lifted her above the more aloof campus prisses and fraternity sweethearts, was that she was right there among us, trudging to class on cold mornings, walking the campus on gray, rainy days, chowing down in the cafeteria with the regular mortals, a goddess among the hapless rabble.

By the second week in February, I was ready to meet a woman like Blondie. I had a thick wad of extra cash, I'd struck up an acquaintanceship with a sophomore in Carolina Residence Hall who agreed to lend me his little French car for five bucks a night, and more importantly, I'd screwed up my courage to the breaking point: I was dead set on landing a date with a girl on campus, or failing that, with at least one of the thousands of females whiling away their lonely lives at Woman's College in Greensboro. I was not going to pass the spring semester wallowing in abject self-pity at the Tap Room.

My big break came on a cold, windy Wednesday night. The guys from second Smith were stuffing their faces at our regular table when I straggled into McEwen Dining Hall and fell in line for my daily fix of meatloaf, peas, mashed potatoes, and gravy. I was running my fingers through my wind-frazzled hair when Blondie turned and smiled. Unbeknownst to me, she'd been standing directly ahead of me in the chow line.

I felt myself teetering on the edge of a life-altering chasm: I could remain as I was, balanced for the foreseeable future in a moribund limbo of beer busts and bull sessions, or I could cast myself into the mystical ether and take the chance of life. Did I have a choice? I drew in a deep breath and uttered the only complete sentence that came into my head: "Gosh, I wonder what kind of swill they'll slop on our plates tonight?"

Her smile faded. "Looks to me like the usual: meatloaf," she said.

"Oh, boy, just what I was hoping for," I responded, calling up a touch of sarcasm as evidence of sophistication. I suspected that was the end of our conversation, but to my amazement, Blondie began chatting away. I could see her delicate, pink-tinted lips moving and the light softening in her blue eyes, but I couldn't comprehend her words. I'd withdrawn into that blissful state of mind a domestic canine enjoys when listening to a human uttering senseless prattle. I smiled and nodded my head, indicating approval of whatever it was she was saying—she might have been telling me to go fetch a bone—but all I was hearing was the sweet music in her voice, a siren's song.

I managed to stagger through the serving line, smiling at whatever Blondie was saying, and then I plodded over to the table where my friends sat stupefied. They stared at me, the grease from their half-eaten meatloaf congealing on their plates.

"Did you just have a conversation with Blondie?" Tindall asked.

I smiled knowingly. "Yeah, I did."

"What did she say?" Gene asked.

"We talked about stuff. You know, nothing in particular."

"Did you ask her out?" Maynard questioned.

"Not exactly."

"You either did or you didn't," Tindall said. "Which is it?"

I was playing it cool. "Let's say I got my foot in the door and let it go at that." And they did.

After two days of gathering my courage, I phoned the second floor of West dorm and asked for Blondie, using her real name, of course. While I waited for her to come to the phone, I considered hanging up—there was still time to spare myself the humiliation of emphatic rejection—and I was about to replace the receiver in its cradle when I heard her say, "Hello."

"Hi," I said cheerfully. "I don't know if you remember me, but I'm the guy who talked with you on Wednesday in the cafeteria. We were discussing the delicious meatloaf." I figured a humorous touch of ironic overstatement wouldn't hurt, thus the use of the adjective "delicious."

Silence. Then she said, "Oh, yeah, I remember. The meatloaf guy. Right."

"Well," I said, taking a more tentative, beseeching tone, "I was wondering if you'd like to go to the Castaways on Saturday night."

Silence.

"I don't know if you've ever been there but I've heard it's a great dance club," I continued, not wanting my invitation to lose its urgency.

"The Castaways," she said. "I love the Castaways."

"We could go this Saturday night if you aren't doing anything."

A contemplative pause. Then she spoke, "It so happens I have no plans for Saturday night. Sure, I'll go. Why not?"

I could hardly credit my luck. I had a date with Blondie. It was obvious she had taken a shine to me during our tête-à-tête in the cafeteria.

"By the way," she said, "what's your name?"

I told her, and she suggested I pick her up at about 7:30 p.m. "Have the housemother call up to the second floor and I'll come right down."

"I'll be there," I said. "See you then." And I hung up before she could change her mind.

After six months on campus, I was the first of our horny coterie to land a date with a living, breathing woman. I hurried to Gene's room, a roguish spring in my step, to tell him my incredible news. I pushed open the door without knocking and found him stretched out on his bunk studying whatever it is business majors study. "You've got to teach me how to dance by Saturday night!" I announced. "I've got a date with Blondie!"

He dropped his book and sat up on the edge of the bed. "You've got a date with Blondie?"

"I do."

"You're lying to me," he said.

"No, I'm not."

"You are," he said again. "You're a damn liar."

"I'm not. I swear. I've got a date with Blondie. She said she'd go out with me to the Castaways."

We persisted with the mock accusations and denials until Gene reluctantly accepted the truth and agreed to instruct me in the subtler points of dancing the Shag. "We'll practice after class on Saturday. It won't take long," he assured me. "A little practice and you'll be dancing like you grew up on Ocean Drive and spent your life at the Pad."

I had no idea what he was talking about—where was Ocean Drive and what was the Pad?—but I knew I'd selected a capable teacher. Gene was indeed a dancing machine; I'd occasionally seen him practicing with a doorknob, and he had the moves down pat.

After months of watching other people dance, I was determined to learn the step for myself.

On Saturday at about 1 p.m., we ran through the fundamentals in Gene's room—"One and two, three and four, five-six-seven-eight," he counted. I studied his every movement as he shuffled back and forth on the grimy linoleum floor. "All right," he said, "we're going to start out on our left foot and it's up and halfway back and up together: one and two, three and four and you'll be back on your right foot. . . ." I stood beside Gene and imitated his steps, shuffling my feet as lithely as possible, but I couldn't quite get the timing right. I was *up* when I should have been *back* or vice versa. I considered myself reasonably coordinated, but it seemed I was physically incapable of following his simple instructions. "Keep your feet close to the floor and remember, you're dancing from the waist down," Gene said, a note of frustration in his voice. "There's no pushing or pulling. The two of you are moving independently but in unison. . . ." He ran through the steps four or five times and then spiced up his moves with a little advanced footwork, which he identified as the drop spin, double kickback, and triple hook. This continued for thirty minutes with no appreciable improvement in my footwork.

"I don't know," I said. "This dance doesn't make sense to me. If you have to concentrate all the time, what fun is it?"

Gene explained the various pleasures one might experience from standing stiff as a fencepost and moving back and forth like a pendulum, but I remained skeptical.

"It's all in the ease of motion," he instructed, "and when the dance is done correctly, trust me, you'll impress your date. Who knows where that will lead?"

I sat down in Gene's desk chair. "You know," I said, "I believe I'm philosophically opposed to dancing the Shag."

"What do you mean?" Gene asked. "There's nothing philosophical about it. It's a dance step."

"Aren't we doing the opposite of what we ought to do when we dance? The idea of dancing is that you move so that you feel good about expressing yourself."

Gene pondered that. "You are expressing yourself, but within the confines of the dance. You're probably overthinking the whole thing. It's not that hard."

"I'm not going to get the step down pat if I can't get my head straight."

"I have an idea," Gene said. "Do you know how to Cha-Cha?"

I'd learned the step in the tenth grade by watching the dancers on the *Buddy Deane Show*. "I can do a good Cha-Cha," I said.

"All right, dance the Cha-Cha, but leave out the side steps and the hip action. Do that and hold one of her hands very gently in yours. You'll be all right."

"That's the Shag?" I asked.

"Nowhere near it," he said. "But it's close enough that no one will notice you aren't doing it correctly . . . except, of course, your date. She'll know, and it'll probably be the last time she goes out with you."

I thanked Gene for his help. "I'll do the best I can," I assured him.

"Do me a favor," he said. "Make a note of the songs the band plays. I'd like to know what they're dancing to at the Castaways these days. Who knows, I might end up there myself."

On Saturday night, forty-five minutes before we turned onto Arnold Street, Blondie, wrapped in her beige overcoat, strolled into the West dorm parlor and surveyed the homogeneous assemblage of guys waiting on their dates, searching for the bonehead dorm rat who had the effrontery to ask her out on a Saturday night.

I'd scored big time: There she was, the preemptive '60s "co-ed," cool and contemplative, her blond hair a halo of spun gold around her delicately proportioned face, her large blue eyes searching the room. She seemed enshrouded in the rosy haze of an imminent sunset, her countenance softened, no doubt, by the 40-watt light bulbs that illumined the room. I could scarcely credit my good fortune. Audacity has its rewards.

"Are you ready to go dancing?" I asked, stepping forward boldly as she entered the lobby.

"Ready all my life," she said, smiling faintly.

• • •

I cut the Renault's engine in the Castaways' parking lot, set the emergency brake, and Blondie and I stepped out into the frozen night, vapor drifting from our mouths. She took my arm, leaning into me gently enough to suggest I was her protector but not so much as to be romantically encouraging, and a minute later we were standing in the club's vestibule. I paid the cover charge of four dollars, and the cashier stamped our hands with an inky indecipherable smudge that entitled us to reenter the club if we decided to step outside for a breath of Arctic air.

If the exterior of the Castaways was commonplace, the interior was celebratory. The blue, red, green, and white of neon beer signs floated in a translucent stratum of cigarette smoke, and the tremulous grumble of energized conversation promised an evening of mysterious delights. Live rock 'n' roll, cold Blue Ribbon, exquisite young women—what more could a feckless freshman ask of life?

A crude, black-skirted stage was pressed into a corner of the front wall, and an electrical strip of stark white spotlights focused on three vocal microphones balanced on upright stainless-steel shafts. A drum kit waited at the back of the platform, and two

Stratocasters and an electric bass rested beside the mikes. A trombone and tenor sax were visible in the far-left corner of the platform, leaning against a ponderous B-3 organ. Amps were stacked high on the sides of the stage, suggesting that the band, whoever they were, intended to play Shea Stadium in the near future. Various utilitarian tables and chairs surrounded the dance floor, a space slightly smaller than a basketball court immediately in front of the band's equipment. The restrooms were at the far end of the building—there was already a short line at the ladies' room—and the bar was distantly visible in the shadows to our immediate left.

The room was about two-thirds full, maybe fifty couples milling about in acrid cancer fumes. We squirmed our way to a convenient table to the left of the dance floor, and Blondie slipped off her coat, revealing a blue wraparound skirt and a red cardigan sweater over a white blouse accented with a gold chain necklace—standard college-girl garb. As she folded her London Fog over a chairback, I realized I hadn't seen her without her overcoat. In the cafeteria or on her way to class, she was shrouded in the same outer garment, a mystery to everyone but herself. But I wasn't disappointed. Beholding her now in the diffused light of the dance floor, clothes seemed a needless extravagance. She was perfectly proportioned, slender and curvy and straight standing.

She smiled at me and immediately signaled the waiter. "I'll have a Blue Ribbon," she called out with the authority of a club regular, which, I suspected, she was. I ordered the same, digging out a couple of bucks to pay the server 75 cents each for the beers, which I thought pricy.

Unfortunately, Blondie wasn't shy about knocking back a brewski. She drained her first bottle in the five minutes it took the gang of musicians to clamber onto the stage and tune their instruments. "I love this place," she said again and ordered a second beer.

The band opened with a rousing rendition of "Hot Cha," a Jr. Walker instrumental featuring a huffy lead sax and a heavy use of cymbals, an altogether infectious tune that crowded the dance floor with couples demonstrating their skill at the Shag. I didn't ask Blondie to dance during the first three or four songs. I needed time to get a feel for the place and its clientele, and I was anxious about my ability to perform the required steps, in my case a feeble bastardization of the Cha-Cha.

As I watched the couples gliding across the dance floor, it was apparent that flaunting one's skill at the Shag was tantamount to a secret handshake between white Southerners. If you didn't know the steps, you weren't part of the in-crowd, so I focused on the dancers' feet as they performed an array of acrobatic contortions, sliding and swiveling this way and that, every sinuous motion effortlessly symmetrical. No doubt one's social status depended on his or her ability to master the more esoteric circumvolutions, and I had to admit that the footwork was astonishing.

Three cold Blue Ribbons brought out the chatterbox in Blondie. I couldn't make out a word she was saying—the Strats were screaming and the drummer was pounding away like a pile driver—so I smiled and nodded. But it occurred to me that I needed to tactfully limit her consumption of alcohol, not because I didn't want her buzzed, a condition that promised unknown late-night delights, but because she was guzzling my pockets. I'd budgeted $10 for the evening—this after shelling out $5 to borrow the Renault—and I had only a reserve $10 bill tucked away in a hidden compartment in my wallet. I'd handed over $4 to the waiter, and we still had two hours to kill. It was time to hit the dance floor, whether or not I made a fool of myself.

As the band struck up a soulful cover of Marvin Gaye's "Stubborn Kind of Fellow," I extended my hand and nodded toward the assemblage undulating in perfect time to the music. Blondie rose from her chair and led me squirming and dodging deep into the crowd of dancers. With my palm down, as per Gene's instructions, I took Blondie's hand gently in mine and stepped back onto my right foot while concentrating on maneuvering my left in the proper direction, and I began to count one and two and three....

That's when Blondie took flight. She yanked her hand from mine and twirled away like an out-of-kilter merry-go-round, lifting one foot and then the other in what appeared to be a frenzied interpretation of the Freddie. Next, she strutted across the dance floor clapping her hands as she lip-synched the words to the song.

As I watched, the simple truth dawned on me: We might be at a club where there was only one acceptable dance step, but if Blondie didn't want to dance the Shag, she didn't have to. She was beautiful, unique, and she didn't give a damn about attracting undue attention. She wasn't there to prove herself to anyone; she was there to have a good time, and she intended to do just that.

I had enough sense to follow her lead. Among my socially inept high school friends I was considered a pretty slick dancer, so I did what I knew. Anyway, no one was watching me; their eyes were on Blondie—and she was flat-out liberating. The Freddie morphed into a free-form rendition of the Jerk/Monkey/Swim, which evolved into a discombobulated rendering of the Dirty Twist. When "Stubborn Kind of Fellow" ended, she danced us into "Hey! Baby" followed by a cover of Shirley and Lee's "Let the Good Times Roll," and we continued nonstop for the next hour. Lordy, how we danced! We were wholly in another dimension, oblivious to the other couples who had to scurry out of our way as we bolted across the dance floor, disrupting their underarm turns and pivots.

When the band took a break—"We're going to catch our breath," the lead singer mumbled into the mike, "and we'll be back in about twenty minutes"—Blondie led me to our table. Her face was crimson with exertion, her golden hair disheveled, damp strands clinging to her cheeks and the nape of her pink neck.

She excused herself. "The girls' room," she whispered, and vanished into the shadows at the back of the club. I collapsed in my chair to catch my breath, rivulets of sweat trickling between my shoulder blades. I drained the warm sluice from my can of Blue Ribbon and took a couple of quick swigs from Blondie's. Recalling my promise to Gene, I unfolded a paper napkin and jotted down a few of the songs the band had played—"Under the Boardwalk," "I'll Be Doggone," "Heat Wave," "My Girl," "It's All Right," "If I Didn't Have a Dime," and "Tracks of My Tears"—and stuffed the folded napkin into the inside pocket of my Harris Tweed sports jacket.

When Blondie returned from her fifteen-minute sojourn in the restroom, she appeared much refreshed. Her cheeks had lost their blush, and her hair, which had been disheveled when last I'd seen her, was tamed by what must have been a determined brushing. She was smiling—that's all I cared about—and she was at ease, whether with me or our circumstance at the Castaways, a club where she apparently felt much at home, I could only guess. She projected an adroitness, a voluble simplicity that was entirely irresistible. I was young enough to appreciate a becoming touch of vanity.

I ordered her another beer and we chatted about the courses she was taking—and that's when I realized she wasn't a freshman. Her classes had 300 prefixes, upper-level sociology, English, art, and economics.

"Are you a sophomore?" I asked.

"A junior," she said.

This was a startling realization. I didn't know of another freshman boy who had dated a junior—in fact, I didn't know of another freshman boy who was dating anyone. Asking out an upperclassman was unheard of, maybe even inappropriate. And suddenly I felt out of my depth and mildly threatened by a woman who was no doubt wiser and more worldly than I. But there was no denying that we were together on a first date at the infamous Castaways, the Home Church of Rock 'n' Roll, celebrating what might be the beginning of a courtship, and she seemed to be having fun. I had no intention of belittling myself in front of her.

"Where are you from?" I asked.

"Richmond," she said. "But my family is moving to Rockville, Maryland, at Easter. My father's taken a job in DC."

I considered telling her about my near disaster on I-95 outside her hometown, but I had sense enough to see myself as she might imagine me, this kid standing on the shoulder of the interstate looking small and stupid and homeless, which of course I'd been on that cold autumn night, so I didn't mention my October debacle.

"Rockville?" I asked. "That's not too far from Annapolis." I'd heard of the town, but I was vague as to its location, except that it was somewhere in the traffic-snarled subdivisions north of DC.

At that moment the sax blasted the intro to "Shotgun" and we danced with renewed frenzy through another hour of the second set. When the band eased into "Unchained Melody"—I couldn't have ordered up a more passionate lyric—Blondie wrapped her arms around my neck, rested her head on my shoulder, and we shuffled through a long embrace. I was hoping she might give herself over to a subtle expression of sexual yearning, but she was, in her temporary state of exhaustion, beyond prurience. When the song ended she let her hands fall from my neck and looked me in the eyes, her face softly accented in the faintly colored lights. "What a stupid, sappy song," she said. "I can't stand it." Then she looked at her watch. "Jesus, it's time to go. I'll get in all kinds of trouble if I'm late getting back to the dorm. I've already gotten locked out twice this year."

Elon girls had to be in by 12:30 a.m. on Saturday nights or they were subject to disciplinary action. A cranky, rotund housemother waited at the dorm's side entrance ready to jot down the name of any girl who wasn't safely locked inside after the porch light had stopped flashing. Blondie hurriedly pulled on her coat, and we were out the door.

I wanted to chat on the drive back so I could bring up the possibility of a second date, but she rested her head on the frosty passenger-side window and instantly fell asleep—or into a sleep-like stupor. As we pulled out of the parking lot onto Arnold Street, I examined again the club's stark façade. I couldn't help but marvel at the shabby industrial inelegance of the low-slung structure that housed so much life and energy, and then I drove west on Route 70.

Safely back in the college parking lot, I woke Blondie. She looked at me bleary-eyed. "What time is it? Are we here?" she asked, a note of alarm in her voice.

"We've got five minutes," I said.

She was instantly out of the car and hurrying to the side entrance of West dorm, with me trailing close behind. As usual on date nights, even when the temperature was below freezing, there were ten or fifteen couples exchanging passionate kisses beneath the oak trees that clustered around the side entrance. We arrived in time to see the porch light flash.

"I had a real good time," Blondie gushed.

"Listen," I said, tentatively, "maybe we can go to the Castaways again soon."

"As far as I'm concerned, we can go every Saturday night until the end of the semester," she said. She gave me a hug, a quick peck on the lips, and melted into a crowd of girls gamboling up the steps and through the open doorway.

I drove the Renault back to Smith dorm and parked. The dimly lighted hallway on the second floor was quiet. I figured the Tap Room boys were fast asleep, but I heard music faintly emanating from Gene's room. I knocked at his door and found him sitting in his boxer shorts on the edge of his bed. He smiled.

"Well?" he asked.

# Fifteen

"Listen. Did you hear that?" Brinkley asked.

I looked up from my history text.

It was Sunday evening, February 20, the day after my third outing with Blondie to the Castaways, where we'd danced more and talked less than we had during our first two visits. I'd stumbled onto the quiet second floor of Smith late Saturday night utterly exhausted and entirely smitten, and I'd spent Sunday afternoon jawing with the guys and describing for Gene the wild dance moves Blondie put down. "Doesn't sound like she's entirely sane," Gene observed. "How do you know she was dancing with you? At least with the Shag, you know who your partner is." Now I was kicked back at my desk focusing on absolute monarchies, constitutionalism in the 1700s, and the evils of rule by something called "aristocratic scions."

"Listen," Brinkley said again.

Brinkley was the best kind of roommate: gone most of the time. He'd arranged his schedule so he could drive home to Virginia on Thursday mornings and return to Elon on Sunday afternoons, which meant he slept in our room only four nights a week.

"What?" I asked.

He held up his open palm to hush me. "Listen to the DJ," he said, inclining his head toward the AM radio glowing on his desk. WBAG was broadcasting a "breaking news story" concerning a plane crash near Alamance Airport. According to the DJ, whose voice was edged with urgency, the pilot and two passengers had died in the crash, and law enforcement and rescue personnel were waiting to hear from the Federal Aviation Agency before removing the bodies from the wreckage. The names of the deceased were being withheld pending the notification of the next of kin. The location of the crash was given as "off Highway 62, near the Alamance Airport."

"All right, let's go," Brinkley said.

"Where?"

"To the airport to see the dead people."

"Why would we do that?"

I wasn't going out of my way to see dead bodies on a cold Sunday night in February. In all my life, I'd never been to a funeral, never stared into an open casket. At the crash site, we might find guts and gore, heads, arms and legs detached from torsos. I felt faint whenever I suffered a paper cut.

"You got anything better to do?" Brinkley asked.

"I don't want to see any dead people, that's for sure. Anyway, I've got to read this chapter."

"Who gives a rat's ass about history? Get up and let's go. Read the damn chapter later."

"You can tell me all about the dead people when you get back."

"What a wimp!"

"I don't want to see any dead bodies!" I said again.

Brinkley grabbed the back of my chair, skidded me away from the desk and caught me by my collar.

"All right, all right," I said. "Don't rip my shirt."

Arguing with Brinkley was always a losing proposition. Once he had his mind set on something, no matter how foolish, he was not to be denied, and he wasn't going to let go of this plane crash business. He rarely asked me to do anything and I suspected that by the time we reached the airport there'd be nothing to see, no dead bodies, no wreckage, nothing. The local rescue personnel would have cleaned up the mess.

"We gotta hurry," Brinkley insisted. "We want to see them remove the bodies."

"All right," I said and pulled on my overcoat.

We clambered down the stairwell and into the dark parking lot. Brinkley fired up his '56 Ford, scratched out onto Haggard Avenue, and hung a hard left on North Williamson to I-85. WBAG was blaring beach music from the dashboard as we traveled through the dark, passing cars that were obeying the speed limit and the occasional big rig that obligingly flashed its headlights in our rearview.

"I hope we get there in time," Brinkley said, stomping on the accelerator. When he spotted the Highway 62 exit, he jammed the gearshift into second, popped the clutch, and the engine backed off, grumbling as we pulled onto a secondary road, the Ford's high beams raking the fallow winter fields.

"How are we going to find the crash?" I asked.

"There'll be lights everywhere—you know, police cars and ambulances and fire trucks. Most of the rescue people in the county will be there. They love this kinda stuff."

I scanned the horizon. No moon. No stars. The sallow illumination from a few scattered one-story houses blurred by us in the dark.

"Look there!" Brinkley barked. "That's got to be it!"

We turned off 62 onto a numberless rural road. A half mile in the distance, whirligigs of color flashed on a low ceiling of clouds, draining any color from the surrounding countryside. As Brinkley slowed the car, I discerned the fixed outline of vehicles parked haphazardly in the distance, their headlights converging on a thicket of dense scrub pine. "That's it," Brinkley said, and he pulled onto the dirt shoulder, angling the Ford into a shallow ditch. "Let's go!"

He cut the ignition, and we jumped out and set off running. Rows of ankle-high corn stubble slapped my pant legs as I stumbled toward the accident site. "Slow down!" I called to Brinkley, but he careened forward as quickly as his legs would carry him.

"Hurry up; it's not much farther!" he yelled, waving me onward.

As we approached the wreckage, human forms were visible, snared in lights mounted on tripods. Five or six men were moving in and out of a wooded area that edged the field, two of them carrying a stretcher covered with a blanket. An aircraft wing, bent and twisted, hung precariously in the limbs of a broken pine.

Brinkley stopped short of entering the zone of light and waited for me to catch up. "Let's see how close we can get," he said in a low voice, and we edged cautiously forward. When we were about thirty feet from the wreckage, a man in a heavy dark overcoat turned and hurried toward us, shining his flashlight in our faces. He was wearing a fedora, the brim creased downward. A lopsided badge was pinned on the breast of his coat. In the indirect illumination, I could make out the lower half of his face, wrinkled and sagging, his mouth a stern line above a prominent chin. "Hold it right there," he said. "Where do you boys think you're going?"

"We want to see the crash," Brinkley said.

"You have no business here. Only emergency personnel are allowed beyond this point." The man paused, then turned and walked toward the colored lights, looking back once over his shoulder, the beam of his flashlight zigzagging into the night sky. Then he dissolved into the disordered bevy of rescue workers. When he was out of earshot, Brinkley said, "We've got to get closer. We aren't going to see any dead bodies from this distance."

"You heard him; we aren't supposed to be here at all."

"Bull," Brinkley said. "He can't tell us what to do."

"I'll wait for you."

"What are they going to do, lock us in jail?"

"Yeah," I said. "They might."

"We aren't breaking any laws," he said, and he began edging closer to the wreckage, tugging me by my coat sleeve as he went. About twenty feet away from the twisted aluminum debris, I could distinguish a crumpled fragment of fuselage and part of the broken propeller lodged in the earth. The tail of the aircraft pointed skyward, and the passenger compartment lay crumpled forward like a discarded accordion. The windshield was shattered, and one of the doors lay detached on the ground, wrenched off its hinges by the impact or by the men who were working to remove the bodies.

"There's one of the dead men," Brinkley said, letting loose of my sleeve.

"Where?"

"Look right there," he said, pointing.

A second stretcher waited beside the wreckage. What I took to be a human torso was hunched into the aircraft's instrument panel, the victim's legs and hindquarters jacked up into the cockpit ceiling.

"Jesus!" Brinkley hissed. "Look at that guy."

I edged forward, straining to see as the rescue workers deliberately eased the body from the torn aluminum. As the victim was lifted outward, his limp right arm caught momentarily on a shard of jagged metal. From my vantage point, it appeared the dead man's pants had been jerked forward by a tremendous force. The back seam of his trousers was split open, exposing the white cloth of his underwear, and his right pant leg was pushed up to his knee, his flesh blinking red, blue, and white in the emergency lights. The workers coaxed the body into position on the stretcher, but the right arm fell loose again, its curled fingers brushing the earth. I could clearly make out the man's pallid face, his features soft and vacant, his open eyes staring skyward. An attendant carefully positioned the arm against the body, a blanket was unfolded above the stretcher, shaken loose, and allowed to float over the dead man's chest and head.

The scene lacked the blood and gore I'd expected. The dead man might have been asleep. He might have lifted himself onto one elbow and spoken to us. Then it hit me: I'm looking at a corpse! I was a few feet away from what was once a living human being.

Brinkley sidled closer to the wreckage, craning his neck to peer into the cockpit. From my position in the dark field, I couldn't determine what was holding his attention, but I heard him gasp, "For Christ's sake! Let's get the hell out of here!"

I didn't need coaxing. I pivoted, stumbled in the soft earth, regained my balance, and set out at a run across the field, retracing my steps with Brinkley close beside me. Neither of us said a word until we reached the road. Then we leaned on the Ford's front fender to catch our breath.

"That was weird," Brinkley said, "you know, with the lights from those trucks and that body getting pulled out of the plane." He paused to collect his wits and added, "The dead man that was left in the cockpit was all mangled up." He stared back at the flashing lights. "Man, it was worse than I could have imagined."

I opened the passenger-side door, slid into the front seat, and tried, without success, to force the image of the dead man's dangling hand and emotionless face out of my brain. Brinkley cranked up the Ford, turned off the radio, and we headed back to the dorm in silence. I was numb, disoriented. Squinting into the high beams of the oncoming traffic, I couldn't help but conjure up a scenario:

Three men, cheerful and eager for a Sunday afternoon adventure, meet in a hangar at the airport to take a short flight in a single-engine aircraft. They joke with one another, laugh. They're confident the little plane will lift into the clouds and return them safely to the earth. After all, thousands of small planes fill the skies on any given day, and accidents only happen to other people, so they climb aboard, chatting about their plans for the coming week—dinner with loved ones, cocktail parties they might attend, reunions with old friends, their lives flush with expectations.

What I couldn't imagine, what wouldn't form in my mind, was the reaction the men might have exhibited as the plane began to plummet, the fuselage twirling and twisting out of control. What did they experience? Did they cry out in fear? Was there one bright horrifying instant when they grasped the fate that was about to befall them?

I knew this much for sure: Until they impacted the earth, their lives held infinite possibilities, years crammed with every imaginable pleasure, all of it ending with absolute finality when the little plane crashed through the trees and smashed into the cold earth. Since I didn't believe in an afterlife and an existence among the angels in heaven, I knew it was the end of all opportunity for happiness for the three unfortunate men, a darkly humorous punch line in the great cosmic joke.

Safely back in our dorm room, I tried to read my history text, but I couldn't muster much concentration. Brinkley turned off the radio and climbed into his bed, pulling the blanket and sheet up to his chin. He rolled over facing the cinderblock wall.

"You know," he said, "I wish we hadn't gone to see those bodies."

"It was a sick thing to do."

"You ever think about dying?"

I told the truth: "Every now and then, but then I tell myself that it's a long ways off."

"Me too. But you never know when and how it will happen, so you oughta have as much fun as possible."

"I guess."

"Yeah," he said, and fell silent.

I closed my history book, shed my pants and shirt, switched off the desk lamp, and climbed into my bunk. I listened to the late-night sounds—the clanking of the radiator, laughter at the far end of the hall, the swoosh of a solitary car passing on Haggard Avenue. I shut my eyes and tried to fall asleep, but I couldn't get the plane crash out of my head, and the more I thought about the dead men, the more my life got all tangled up with theirs. It was unfair. A universe that treats us benevolently at one moment can turn fatally malevolent the next. One wrong decision, however trivial, could lead to oblivion.

Brinkley and I might have been killed on I-85 while driving back to the dorm. A semi might have swerved into our lane and sent the Ford tumbling down the interstate, our bodies flung like ragdolls onto the asphalt. Then our corpses would be placed on stretchers, loaded into an ambulance, and taken to the morgue. My parents would get a phone call, and they'd be left to wonder why I'd been traveling the highway on a Sunday night in February. "What could he have been doing out at that hour?" my tearful mother would ask. My parents would never know about the plane crash and the dead bodies and the futility of it all.

. . .

On Tuesday evening, I stopped by the library to read the Monday edition of *The Daily Times-News*. Above the fold on the front page the headline blared: "Three Die In Alamance Plane Crash." A close-up black-and-white photograph of the wrecked aircraft was surrounded by a lengthy article, which supplied the details of the accident. The pilot was a salesman for a company in Lumberton that manufactured the single-engine plane and an autopsy had been ordered on his body. He might have suffered a heart attack or a stroke. The other two victims were locals, both in their thirties. A witness described the plane as "spinning straight down" into the ground and said that the crash sounded like "dynamite exploding."

The deaths had warranted a front-page story in a small-town newspaper, but I knew that in a day or two the three dead men would be forgotten by everyone but their grieving families, that life in the little town of Burlington would go on as if nothing had happened. That's the way it had to be. It was a brief, sad commentary on the tenuousness of life.

Immediately below the plane crash article was an AP story about the war in Vietnam that focused on the number of Americans who had died in recent helicopter crashes. It contained strange place-names, Da Nang and Hue among them. When no one was looking, I surreptitiously tore off the front page of the newspaper, folded it into my notebook, and returned what was left of the paper to its place on the periodical rack. Then I walked out alone into the night.

Death was all around me. Death in Vietnam, death in airplane crashes, death on the highways. Sometimes perfectly healthy people dropped dead for no discernable reason. In high school, teenagers killed in car crashes were as ubiquitous as cancer uncles, and already an Elon freshman like myself had died in a car accident as he rode from the Tap Room back to the college. Of this much I was certain: life was out to get me.

# Sixteen

"It's not fair," Blondie yelled, leaning across the wobbly table, an empty Blue Ribbon can rolling into my lap.

On the last Saturday night in March, the Castaways was slammed. The house band, whose lead singer was croaky and sweat-soaked from belting out a wicked thirty-minute Wilson Pickett rendition of "Mustang Sally," had taken a break, and now the crowd was Shagging to a little truth from the jukebox.

It had taken six dates and a considerable chunk of my Drug Fair money, but Blondie and I had achieved a clumsy, semi-romantic familiarity by talking for hours about nothing in particular. During the thirty-minute rides from the college to the outskirts of Greensboro and back, I told lies about my buddies on second Smith and their endless hijinks, and she chattered away about her friends in Virginia Dorm and their amorous entanglements. We didn't discuss our plans for the future—Lord knows, I had none—and we never talked politics or religion or anything that might require a modicum of thought.

Talk didn't matter. I'd been smitten with Blondie's unaffected grace since I'd first spoken with her in the cafeteria, and six weeks into our relationship, I was fixated on her less obvious attributes, those insignificant gestures that lifted her above the typically beautiful. She was always smiling, steadfastly optimistic, and when she laughed, which was often, she tilted her head up and back, and tiny quarter moons formed at the corners of her mouth. If I made a joke, however asinine, she'd lean forward and rest a hand gently on my forearm, which I took as a sign of affection. Gone was the dervish-like twirling that had spirited her across the floor on our first date to the Castaways. Now she was less animated, more expressive, moving her shoulders almost imperceptibly, arms extended, her eyes closed as she lip-synched the words to each song. Her flaxen hair, which had never shown signs of being coiffured, was wilder, unkempt oodles of tangled curls cascading onto her shoulders and across her face as we danced. A dab of feverish powder brightened her cheeks, but she'd abandoned eyeliner and lipstick altogether.

"What's not fair?" I asked, as the jukebox offered up a breezy beach tune. She didn't answer but grabbed my hand, pulling me into the crowd. An hour of hard dancing had worn me flat out, but I couldn't deny Blondie anything. We zigzagged between the swaying couples to occupy a tiny space in the center of the dance floor.

"Now," she said, still holding my hand firmly, "let's do this stupid dance." She began to shuffle up and back in what I took to be a parody of the Shag. I followed, recalling Gene's instructions about dancing the Cha-Cha. We were doing it all wrong—the Cha-Cha and the Shag—but no one noticed, and we laughed at ourselves. "I think you've got it," she whispered, her lips warm against my ear. "Now you're an honest-to-God grit."

There was more truth than irony in what she said. I was beginning to feel myself a Southerner. As my post-Christmas return to the college had inspired in me a sense of homecoming, I now felt an affinity with the other dancers at the Castaways. I sang along with the lyrics to each beach tune, and I knew the names of the Saturday night regulars who staked out private slices of the dance floor. When the best Shaggers in the Triad were in attendance, the word was passed along to Blondie and me: "Spider's in the house," or "Danny B will be dancing tonight." Although I still longed to hear the Stones and the Beatles and the Spoonful, I was, nominally, a member of the club, a Castaways regular who felt himself safely grounded in the South, even if I didn't own a pair of Nettletons or an alligator belt.

Bob Collins' "If I Didn't Have a Dime," Blondie's favorite beach tune ("If you weren't standing there, ruby lips and golden hair..."), clanked from the jukebox, and she segued into the more esoteric steps Gene had suggested I learn—the triple hook and the apple jack—executing reasonable facsimiles of each. Anyone watching her would have sworn she'd been Shagging all her life. I struggled to follow her elegant stepping, but I was as awkward as ever, twisting in one direction as she turned in another, fumbling along a beat or two behind her.

"What's unfair?" I asked between tunes.

"What are you talking about?"

"You said something was unfair. What is it?"

"Oh, yeah," she said, "the dancing. It's not fair to dance like that." And she motioned toward the couples stepping out to whatever 45 was spinning on the turntable.

I wasn't sure what she meant by "unfair," but I didn't need to know. "When did you learn the Shag?" I asked.

"I'm faking it," she said. "You can get away with anything if you're just a little bit smart."

Worn down by way too much fun, we left the Castaways early that evening, hurrying beneath the vapor lights on Arnold Street, our coat collars pulled up against the chill. The Renault was, as usual, slow to warm up, and we shivered, our breath icing on the windows.

"I'm ready for spring," I said. "It's been cold for a long time."

"Yeah, it seems like long," Blondie said, huddling against me.

As we drove east on Highway 70, we listened to the midnight news on WBAG. The DJ listed the cities where anti-war demonstrations had taken place that day—Chicago, Boston, Washington, and San Francisco. In New York, 20,000 protesters had marched down Fifth Avenue.

"If you get drafted, are you going to go?" Blondie asked.

The question took me by surprise. We'd never discussed the war or the draft.

"I haven't given it much thought," I said. "I plan on keeping my 2-S deferment."

"What if you lose it?"

"I'll deal with that when and if the time comes," I said, and then paused. "My father would like me to join the army so the government will pay my tuition when I get out."

"*If* you get out. Boys like you are getting killed in Vietnam every day. Read the papers."

"The guys who are serving in Vietnam either flunked out of school or volunteered because they thought the war would be a big adventure." I believed what I was saying.

"Guys are getting drafted out of the classroom and deposited in a country on the other side of the world. I wouldn't want that to happen to you."

This was a side of Blondie I'd not experienced. She actually had a political opinion. "I didn't know you cared about the war."

"I think about it," she said, and paused. "What are you trying to say?"

"Nothing, I was just—"

"I have another friend who's about to get drafted," she continued. "I worry about him, too."

This was the first she'd made mention of another suitor, which I took "a friend" to mean, and a pang of insecurity left me momentarily speechless. "There's nothing we can do about the war," I said, finally. I didn't need to become entangled in a discussion about another boyfriend, which would undoubtedly end unhappily for me, but I couldn't resist asking. "Is this friend someone you're involved with?"

"Involved with? Whatever do you mean by that?"

"You know, someone you're serious about. A boyfriend?"

"Serious? I'm not serious about anyone in particular, and you're my boyfriend for now."

"Well, then, is there someone other than me you'd rather go dancing with?" The phrasing of my question instantly struck me as stilted, but Blondie knew exactly what I meant and she laughed, shaking her blond curls.

"I never dance with any one guy. I just dance. I love to dance. And I love the Castaways when you take me there for a good time." There was an innocent cheerfulness in her honesty, her noncommittal answer, and I couldn't help but smile. Like everything about her, her carefully chosen words were wholly disarming. "You know what I like about you?" she asked, touching my cheek with her cold fingertips. "You're fearless. You walked right up to me in the cafeteria and starting griping about how bad the food was. What could be more romantic than that?"

We both laughed as I pulled the Renault into the parking lot beside Virginia Dorm. I walked her to the side door where the dreaded housemother waited, and we kissed good night under the orange porch light.

"Next Saturday," she said, and disappeared into the dark hallway at the top of the stairs. Blondie was more than a little bit smart.

# Seventeen

The Easter holidays commenced with the close of classes on Wednesday, April 6. I caught a ride north with a churlish upperclassman who charged $10 a head, stuffing six of us (not counting himself) into his Dodge station wagon—three in the front seat, three in the back seat, and one discomfited passenger sandwiched between our luggage and the tailgate—raking in a total of $60 when gas costs 27 cents a gallon. We set out after lunch and made it as far as Dinwiddie, Virginia, where he was pulled over for speeding by a sheriff's deputy driving a pickup truck and forced to pay $50 to a magistrate running a scam out of a dilapidated gas station. As soon as we resumed our trip, the dashboard generator light flashed red a couple of times and then glowed continuously. We coasted into a filling station near Petersburg, where a mechanic installed new brushes for the generator. The repair took an hour and cost another $25, and I began to entertain the possibility that there is, after all, justice in the universe.

It was dark when the driver dropped me in Glen Burnie. I called my father collect from a pay phone near the Harundale Mall. It took him forty-five minutes to make the trip from Annapolis, and when he pulled onto the shoulder of the road flashing his high beams, I didn't recognize the car he was driving. Gone was our sensible Ford Fairlane station wagon with its faux-wood paneling, and in its place the old man was behind the wheel of a brand-new lemon-yellow Buick LeSabre. It was the biggest and most luxurious automobile I'd ever seen him drive, and, wonder of wonders, it was a ragtop!

I shouldn't have been surprised; my father had a weakness for convertibles. Immediately after World War II, he purchased a used '35 Chevy drop-top, and when I was four years old he acquired a new 1950 Crosley slide-back convertible, which resembled a refrigerator mounted on tiny wheels. But from 1951 until I entered college, we'd owned sensible family cars—a desperately underpowered Falcon station wagon that struggled to climb the twelve percent grade on the north side of the Severn River Bridge, a Buick Special my mother accidentally smashed through the garage door, four or five Chevys, including a gold, teeth-rattling '58 Chevy station wagon with bad kingpins, a Rambler Custom whose passenger-side door had a habit of flying open when my father took a hard left turn, a powder-blue, plain-Jane '55 Ford that chuffed black smoke like a steam locomotive, and other jalopies I've long since forgotten.

As I marveled at the gleaming LeSabre idling on the shoulder of Rt. 2, it occurred to me that I might, if adequately ingratiating, borrow the new car for a quick trip to Rockville, where I'd squire Blondie around town with the top down. I was gauche enough to believe that the sight of the shiny new convertible might subtly enhance and secure my relationship with Blondie. I was certain that tooling around rural North Carolina in a borrowed Renault Dauphine wasn't doing me much good.

I tossed my suitcase into the back of the LeSabre and slipped into the shotgun seat. "Jeez," I said, "nice car!"

My father pushed a chrome button on the dashboard, and the black cloth top folded neatly into the boot, the dusky cosmos gradually revealing itself above us. I stared skyward into a universe of stars twinkling through the smog from the Sparrows Point steel mills. We pulled into traffic and the old man wound her up to 65 mph, pressing me back into my seat as the automatic transmission shifted smoothly through the gears. Long and sumptuous, the LeSabre floated on a cushion of air.

Despite his new ride, my father was in an obstinate mood: he refused to buckle his seat restraint. The fasten-your-seat belt alarm squawked incessantly. Add to this cacophony the wind and road noise and the AM radio tuned to a station blaring one Frank Sinatra recording after another and it wasn't long before our ride south on Ritchie Highway was transformed from a sporty road trip through a chilly spring evening into the kind of psychological torture human rights organizations would find abhorrent.

My homecoming went unnoticed. My redheaded brother was bouncing around the house guzzling Cokes and stuffing Utz potato chips into his freckled face, and Debbie was arguing with our mother about the latest disreputable boyfriend.

When I awakened on Saturday, April 7, my mother insisted I hurry down to the Safeway to beg Mr. Short for a summer job, a task for which I had no enthusiasm. "I'll tell you this," she said, "you aren't going to spend the summer stretched out on the couch watching that asinine *Where the Action Is!*"—Dick Clark's current music extravaganza featuring Paul Revere and the Raiders and the scrumptious Linda Scott. The half-hour program had been on network TV for about a year, and I was fond of lusting over the go-go dancers and hearing the latest rock 'n' roll hits. But my mother was, as always, emphatic, and there was no point in delaying the inevitable. I hoofed it to the Safeway, where I found my old boss huddled in his office making out the work schedule for the coming week. He was pleased to see me, shook my hand hard, and rehired me on the spot. "I can always use a good cashier," he said.

I winced.

"I've got people going on vacation," he continued, "and you can fill in, maybe work a couple of weeks of night stock to give those guys a break." He paused. "The manager at Drug Fair said you did a bang-up job at Christmas."

After lunch, my father returned from the Academy and stayed the afternoon to paint the new sheetrock in the rec room an obnoxious shade of blue labeled "Robin's Egg." I dreaded working with the old man. He was short-tempered and sullen and tended to blame every minuscule mistake on my "inability to concentrate," a criticism that was certainly justified.

"Look, you're leaving holidays all over the place," he said. "Make sure you get good coverage with your roller. And wipe up those spills before they dry on the floor."

"I don't like this color," I said. "It looks cheap."

"It is cheap," he said. "Buy one gallon, get two gallons free."

I tried to keep in mind that my father had suffered a grim childhood with my alcoholic grandfather—Grandmother Drager's "good man gone wrong"—who felt obliged to rough up his wife and kids when he'd had a few too many, which was whenever he managed to get his hands on a bottle of hooch. Grandfather Smith was an inveterate gambler, and he'd taught my father to box so he could enter him in tournaments in the Akron area where boys twelve and older would slug it out while adults wagered on the outcome of each match. My grandfather made a pile of money betting that my father could beat the snot out of every other kid his age.

On one particularly gruesome occasion, my father, who was only thirteen at the time, had two bouts in one afternoon. In the first, he suffered a broken nose, but he won the match on points. Before my father's second bout, my grandfather sneaked over to the opposite corner and whispered to the unsuspecting challenger, "If you want to beat that Smith kid, hit him as hard as you can right in the schnozzola." When the bell sounded, my father took a right cross to his broken nose, making him so angry he knocked his opponent out cold. My grandfather had wagered a sizable sum on the unconscious kid, and he went home penniless—and thirsty. That night he got drunk and whipped my father with an electric cord. My grandfather loved to tell this story, laughing boisterously when he blurted the punch line: "I gave your old man one hell of a licking that night!" It was no wonder my father was moody. Still, it didn't make him any easier to get along with.

So I slapped on the cheap Mary Carter paint and tried to keep my mouth shut. When we'd finished the job, I took the opportunity to ask, "If I wash and wax the car, could I use it to go out on a date one night?"

My father glared at me and said nothing, which I took as an emphatic no.

On Friday morning, I read John Galsworthy's "The Apple Tree," which Professor Gerow, my English 112 professor, had assigned before we departed for the holidays. It was a terrible story, and I had to force myself to finish the assignment. That afternoon I walked to the city dock and up Main Street to Pete's Pool Hall. I'd hoped to find a few of my high school friends loitering around the billiard tables, but there wasn't a familiar face among the hard cases racking balls and chalking cues, so I cut across State Circle past the statue of the notorious Judge Taney and the ancient state Capitol and wandered over to the St. John's campus. The Maryland spring was a few weeks behind the season in North Carolina, and the campus trees—including the last surviving Liberty Tree—laced a stitching of green against a blue sky.

After supper I slipped into the family room to admire the new paint job and ended up sitting on the couch with my father to watch the *CBS Evening News.* That night's featured report concerned the increasingly fierce fighting in Vietnam, accompanied by grainy black-and-white film footage of the mangled bodies of Vietcong piled haphazardly in a jungle-rimmed field following an attack on an American firebase.

"Have you given any thought to going into the service?" my father asked.

We'd had this conversation many times, and I was in no mood to discuss my possible enlistment in the army, especially when Uncle Walter was announcing the number of Americans killed in action the previous week. "No," I answered immediately.

"Maybe you should."

"Why would I do that?"

"Might be good for you. I talked with Bob Barnes last week, and your friend Barrie loves the army."

"He does?" I still wasn't buying that pile of bunkum.

"Bob said Barrie's lost weight, he's in great shape, and he's training in Hawaii."

My father had been stationed in Honolulu during World War II, and he was fond of recalling the days he'd spent lounging on Waikiki Beach with his navy buds. "You'd like Hawaii."

"I like where I am right now."

"If you went into the service, you'd have your education paid for when you got out."

That's when it occurred to me that the new Buick LeSabre, which I'd thought might be a boon to my social life, was going to gobble up what little allowance I had coming. My parents had to make car payments on their fancy new ride, and the cash had to come from an already tight family budget.

"I enjoyed the military," he continued. "It's a great experience; you'll meet lots of interesting people."

An army officer holding a clipboard was counting bodies, pointing randomly into a tangle of black-and-white corpses piled high on the flickering cathode-ray tube.

"I don't know why we're in Vietnam. I mean, what's the point?" As soon as I'd spoken those words, I knew I was in trouble.

My father responded angrily. "You've got it pretty damn easy sitting on your butt while other kids your age are fighting for their country."

I hated it when the old man got on one of his self-righteous patriotic jags. A hundred times he'd told me how he'd joined the navy on December 8, 1941, when he was flush with patriotic fervor. But I also knew the truth concerning his military service. I'd once asked what he'd done in the war, and he'd confessed to purposely avoiding combat. He and other college and professional athletes spent the war staging boxing smokers on ships in port for R&R.

"I'm not sitting on my butt," I said.

"Yeah, well, I call it 'sitting on your ass,'" he replied, inserting "ass" for emphasis and upping the ante. He was hot. "You've got it pretty damn easy, I'll tell you that."

"My grades were good last semester." Then I said it: "You have to admit that I wasn't home by Thanksgiving like you predicted."

He turned his head quickly to stare at me, surprised that I'd overheard the offhand remark he'd made to my mother on the afternoon he'd deposited me at Elon. The old man didn't like being wrong.

I got up from the couch. "I've got reading to do," I said. And added a parting shot, "This Vietnam stuff sounds like a complete waste to me."

"Yeah, well, give the military some thought," my father called out as I started up the stairs. "It might be that you'll have no choice in the matter."

• • •

On Tuesday, April 12, I caught the Greyhound south through a greening countryside whose landmarks had grown familiar during the preceding nine months. I anticipated Virginia's killing fields—Bull Run, Fredericksburg, Chancellorsville, and Spotsylvania—and I whispered the Native American names for the rivers we crossed—Mattaponi, Pamunkey, Rappahannock. A few hours into the trip we rolled beneath the clock tower at the Richmond Main Street Station and rumbled across the James River Bridge. South of the old Confederate capital, I caught a passing glimpse of the Philip Morris offices where I'd stood for seven hours, abandoned and desperate, the previous October.

At Petersburg we boarded passengers, and a pimply, red-headed Duke junior toting a stack of books squirmed into the seat next to me. As we jolted south on old US 1, rumbling down the main streets of dying Southern towns—DeWitt, South Hill, Henderson, Oxford, Creedmoor—my seatmate, a theology major wired on bennies, discoursed incessantly on the philosophers he'd been studying. He began with Boethius, reading from Chaucer's translation of *The Consolation of Philosophy*, not one word of which I understood, and ended three hours later with passages from Kierkegaard's *Concluding Unscientific Postscripts to Philosophical Fragments*, which might as well have been written in Middle English. By the time he bounced off the bus in Durham, I was way beyond contemplating the abstract. "Promise me you'll read Kierkegaard," he called out before stepping off the bus.

"Sure thing," I yelled back.

I considered finishing my history reading as we rolled west on I-85, but Theology Boy had fried my cerebrum. There was nothing to do but stare out the grimy bus window at the thickening Southern foliage that threatened to swallow up everything that strayed beyond the shoulder of the road.

We arrived at the bus station in Burlington at 8 p.m., and I shared a cab to the college with a couple of upperclassmen. The second floor of Smith was dead quiet when I stepped from the stairwell into the dark hall. The semester would end in three weeks, and the dorm already seemed to lack the energy that had sustained me during the previous months. Where was the music? The raucous laughter? The persistent banter of friends?

Alone in my room—Brinkley wouldn't return until the following morning—I lay in the gloom wondering why I couldn't remain as I was. I had no desire to return to Annapolis for the summer. The thought of living at home with my exasperating family was anything but cheering, and I cringed when I considered the likelihood that I'd soon be pounding on a cash register ten hours a day at the Eastport Safeway. But I had no car or job in North Carolina and couldn't sustain myself without transportation and money. Moreover, my Drug Fair stash was diminishing at an alarming rate. Tossing about in my bed, I realized what was the matter, what would always be the matter: I was afraid of change, especially when that change would put an end to a decidedly satisfying period of my young life. But I understood, too, that I was powerless to stay the passage of time, that I couldn't delay what was coming, whatever it was. I switched on the desk lamp and tried reading about the Battle of Wissembourg, but it was hopeless. I couldn't focus, and it wasn't until the early hours of the morning that I dozed off.

Nevertheless, I was on time for my 8 a.m. lecture, diligently scribbling notes and jotting down the irritating details of Easter break. I was determined not to miss any classes during the remainder of the semester, and I resolved to use my afternoons typing up summaries of my professors' lectures as study guides for exams. The best way to mitigate my father's insistence that I join the military was to make the dean's list, which was a real possibility. If I had a solid B average, he couldn't refuse to send me back to college in the fall. What would he say to his friends: "Stephen was making good grades, but we thought he'd be better off wading through a rice paddy in Southeast Asia"?

The only assignment I had yet to complete was an essay on some obscure aspect of Galsworthy's "The Apple Tree." I had a C average in Professor Gerow's class, but I needed at least a B for a final grade. To do that, I had to earn an A on the final essay. Then I'd have to ace the exam.

As for my other courses, I was up-to-date on my reading, and my lecture notes were thorough enough. History and political science weren't a worry. Religion required that I memorize Dr. Sloan's text, which was no problem, and my notes from Health were detailed. I could only hope I didn't have to identify any of the slides I'd avoided during most of the semester—all those disgusting photos of ulcerated body parts and chests and abdominal cavities splayed open at autopsy! Jesus, spare me....

I had a solid B in Economic Geography and a B+ in Selected Topics in Physical Science, a bubblehead course I'd signed up for to avoid the more traditional physics or biology courses, which were, for me at least, real brain strainers.

• • •

Despite my determination to study hard and make the dean's list, I was distracted by the soft warmth that settled over the Piedmont. The blossoming ornamental pears on Trollinger Avenue had peaked, their white petals drifting into the withering forsythia blooms lining the railroad tracks adjacent to the campus, and the grass in the commons in front of West dorm had renewed itself. The oaks and sycamores were in full leafage.

On the night of Saturday, April 23, Blondie and I hit the Castaways, drank a couple of quick Blue Ribbons, and danced for an hour. We left the club early and drove to a golf course south of Burlington, where we rolled around on the seventh green for an hour. The night air was mild as milk, and we were both buzzed. I'd left the windows down on the Renault and the radio on, allowing top twenty hits to waft through the soft spring night. Clusters of white azaleas and dogwood shone luminously in the dark, and a light wind rustled the trees that dotted the fairway. Above us the dome of stars rolled on and on, impassive but persistent.

It was a custom-made moment, worth an entire year of studying, worth my slaving away the Christmas holidays at Drug Fair, worth all the worrying and wangling, worth everything. We were floating above the Southern countryside. I even took a momentary liking to Sam the Sham and the Pharaohs' "Li'l Red Riding Hood," a tune so juvenile I felt a trifle embarrassed when the lyric carried our way. Sam the Sham was followed by the unmistakable dada-da-dada-da of a shuffling electrified C chord that introduced the lyric—"What a day for a daydream...." From the first note, I had this notion that "Daydream" was a song that had been wandering the universe forever, and that the writer had merely snatched it from thin air. After overdosing on "Hang on Sloopy," "Hurt So Bad," and "I Love Onions" in the fall of '65 and early '66, this bouncy stripped-down ditty was exhilarating and in perfect keeping with my infatuation with the Carolina spring. What could be more appropriate than falling on your face on somebody's new-mowed lawn? What followed was "Double Shot (of My Baby's Love)," a lyric I might have written myself. "Double Shot" was a drunken keg party featuring a chorus of frat boys egged on by a cymbal-based backbeat.

I couldn't comprehend how it had happened—it wasn't the result of any tender manipulation on my part—but Blondie and I had gotten easy with each other. There was none of the genuine intimacy, physical or otherwise, that accrues from years of familiarity, but it was close enough. We walked hand-in-hand back to the car. I turned off the radio, and we drove along roads on the very rim of the world. The South was singing to us. It was the sweetest music I'd ever heard.

# Eighteen

"Ain't gonna happen," Brinkley said.

"What's that?" I asked.

"If you're expecting an A or a B on an essay in Gerow's class, you won't get it." He was leaning over my shoulder as I sat at my desk, studying the single sentence I'd managed to scribble in my notebook during the twenty minutes I'd been focusing on the first draft of my essay on John Galsworthy's "The Apple Tree."

"If I don't come up with a decent topic, I'm going to get an F, that's for sure."

"What story are you writing about?"

"'The Apple Tree.'"

"Never heard of it."

"You're lucky."

"Doesn't make any difference what story it is, nobody gets an A or B on a Gerow essay."

I looked up into Brinkley's angular, smiling face. "I got a B on my *Gatsby* essay."

"You must be Shakespeare," he said.

I'd first laid eyes on Betty Gerow when she stepped in front of our English 112 class on the second floor of the Alamance Building at 1 p.m. on Monday, February 2. She was an inconspicuous middle-aged woman whose out-of-date dark-frame glasses magnified her roundish, piercing eyes. She did not greet our class with a warm, toothy smile, but neither was she the badass English professor of freshman lore—which is to say that she was no Tully Reed. However, she laid down the law in the first five minutes of that first class: a tardy counted as an absence, and five absences would result in the student receiving an F in the course. When she began lecturing on a literary topic, which occurred exactly six minutes into that first meeting, she demanded our attention, explicating in detail the thematic subtleties of *The Great Gatsby*. If she had a fault, it revealed itself in later classes: a propensity for requiring outlandish reading assignments. "Read *Daisy Miller* for Wednesday," she'd say without a hint of irony, and the following class period, she'd expose a slacker by asking him a question that was impossible to answer if he hadn't thoroughly completed the reading assignment.

"Why does Winterbourne find Eugenio impertinent?" Any student unable to supply the correct answer was humiliated and likely dropped the class, his or her name repeated during roll call for the remainder of the semester, a warning that her classroom was no place for an idler. By the middle of April, the original complement of thirty students was down to twelve determined souls, and I'd only managed to hang on by completing readings well ahead of time.

I'll give Gerow this: She was even-tempered, inspiring in me neither fear nor affection. And she taught me much that Tully Reed had not: how to write a decent topic sentence, how to organize an essay using a rough outline, how to arrange quotation marks in relation to other punctuation marks, how to avoid plagiarism, and how to complete a probing, systematic revision. What she didn't teach me, even though it was probably her primary objective, was how to think, how to unclog my cluttered brain, how to rework and polish an idea and see it through to an agreeable conclusion—thus my predicament as I sat at my desk in my dorm room struggling to come up with a workable thesis for an essay.

"I hate this story," I told Brinkley.

"Maybe that's what you should write," he suggested.

"What?"

"I hate this story. That's your first sentence."

"You know, that's not a bad idea."

"Explain to me what happens in the story," Brinkley said, feigning interest.

I couldn't *explain* "The Apple Tree" to anyone. I'd been an avid reader since elementary school, and I'd learned early on that it's impossible to *explain* a piece of literature to another human being. At the beginning of the semester, a shirker in Gerow's class had asked me, "What's *The Great Gatsby* about?" and I'd answered, "It's the story of a guy who throws big parties in hopes his ex-girlfriend will show up." It was a pretty good one-sentence synopsis, but it didn't *explain* the story, and it didn't help the student answer questions when Gerow began to probe the class. He was a goner. By way of assuaging Brinkley's phony curiosity I might have said, "'The Apple Tree' is the story of an elderly Englishman who discovers the grave of a long-lost love with whom he might have lived a happy and fulfilling life if class differences hadn't intervened," but his eyes would have glazed over—and rightly so.

"It's a silly story with a stupid ending" was all I could manage.

"Well, write about that."

"All right, I will." And I closed my notebook, turned off my desk lamp and hit the sack.

When I returned from class the following afternoon, I set to work using Brinkley's suggestion, writing in pencil on spoiled

213

sheets of erasable bond. The assignment had been announced to the class on April 25 with a due date of May 2, so I'd had adequate time to mull over my intent and six days to write and polish the final essay.

With my topic and thesis firmly in mind, the words flowed. I employed Twain's "The Literary Offenses of Fenimore Cooper," which we'd read and discussed earlier in the semester, as a model, enumerating Galsworthy's various transgressions, which were, I believed, legion. First, the story was overwritten. I'd read *Look Homeward, Angel*, which was wordy, but "The Apple Tree" was a toxic word dump. Galsworthy never passed up an opportunity to say in a thousand words what he might have said in ten—and worse, he was a show-off, a literary snob, padding his narrative with obscure literary allusions that I lacked the time and ambition to investigate. Second, the storyline was hopelessly sentimental, like a sappy old Lassie movie with the worse-for-wear collie limping home from misfortunes that would put Odysseus' journey to shame. Third, his characters lacked verisimilitude. Borrowing directly from Twain, I stated that the reader should be able to tell the dead characters from the living and that the characters ought to say and do what living people do, even if they appear to be dead. More than anything else, the story wasn't true to life and had nothing to offer a freshman boy who considered dancing the Hully-Gully the ultimate intellectual activity. On and on I went, ladling up the criticism as if I were a scholar writing for the *New York Review of Books*. I showed no mercy, quoting liberally to illustrate my grievances and not mentioning a single positive element of the story.

It never once occurred to me that I was on the low side of the learning curve, and I scribbled for three hours until I had at least twenty-five hundred words of jumbled accusations against

Galsworthy. Then I arrived at the story's conclusion. No doubt I was caught up in a Thoreauvian celebration of the Southern spring—but I wasn't falling for Galsworthy's sappy ending. It was way more than I could endure: "And before his eyes, dim with tears, came Megan's [his deceased lover's] face with the sprig of apple blossom in her dark, wet hair. . . . Spring, with its rush of passion, its flowers and song—the spring in his heart . . ." I could hear the simpering violins. The ending was easy meat, and I took the author to task for manipulating his audience with blatant sentimentality. All that bathos set against the gloriously redemptive power of renewal was a waste of verbiage which, if employed correctly, might have generated genuine emotion. I ended my essay with the audacious suggestion that "The Apple Tree" be banished forthwith from the literary canon on grounds of gross corniness.

Working steadily, I completed my first draft at 5 p.m. on April 25, and believed that my essay was well on its way to rescuing me from the possible discomfiture of relocating to Southeast Asia. I had an entire week to complete my rewrite and make a fair copy in longhand (typing the essay on my Olivetti would require too much time and effort, given my abysmal typing skills). I was feeling good and happily complacent, so much so that I took the next three days off to read for my other courses and drink beer at the Tap Room.

On Saturday morning I phoned Blondie and begged off on our standing date. I needed the time, I told her, to put the final touches on my essay. Truth be known, I was down to $32 of Drug Fair money, and I still had to pay someone to drive me home at the end of the semester. "I've got this important essay to finish," I told her. "We'll make it next Saturday for sure." With exams a couple of weeks away, she had her own work to complete, including a research paper for an economics course in which she was struggling.

I spent Saturday afternoon tinkering with my second draft, correcting the order in which my paragraphs were arranged so that the most convincing piece of evidence led to my conclusion, as Gerow had taught me. Convinced that my organization was effective, I reviewed the story's details, toying with a couple of alternative conclusions, neither of which pleased me. And that's when I suffered a fortuitous insight. As I was rereading the final chapter of "The Apple Tree," it came to me that Galsworthy's writing bore a striking resemblance to the prose of P.G. Wodehouse, whose comic novels I almost knew by heart. I still had my copy of *The Brinkmanship of Galahad Threepwood* in my desk drawer. I opened it to a random chapter and compared the prose to one of Galsworthy's stilted passages. And there it was, plain as day: P.G. Wodehouse was parodying John Galsworthy! The ineffectual, highborn protagonist, the poor ingenuous farm girl who falls hopelessly in love with someone above her station in life, the bucolic English countryside, the overly dramatic focus on the trivial. Even unimportant details were consistent—Wodehouse's dimwitted Lord Emsworth, his prize-winning sow, the Empress of Blandings (Galsworthy's story featured an errant hog), the confusion occasioned by misapprehended love—each had parallels in "The Apple Tree." I was on to something. I rewrote my conclusion to state that Galsworthy's story was so banal that P.G. Wodehouse couldn't resist outright lampoonery. It was, I thought, the zinger I needed, proof that I was a critical reader.

Convinced I'd written the perfect Gerow essay, I closed my notebook before dinner and stepped out with the guys to the cafeteria for Saturday night steak and potatoes. Tindall had driven his family's Dodge Polaris convertible back to Elon after Easter break, and as we chowed down, he, Gene, Maynard, and I decided to catch a movie at the Starlight, a down-at-the-heels drive-in on

Highway 87 where we occasionally viewed cheesy Russ Meyer films that flashed across a lopsided screen.

I reasoned that a few laughs with the guys would provide some objectivity regarding my Galsworthy masterwork. No doubt I'd awaken Sunday morning with a clear head and fresh perspective that would inspire a few flourishes to my treatise.

The title of the low-budget production inflicted upon us that spring night is long since lost to memory—with any luck the film, cultural artifact that it was, has vanished as well—but I recall that the female lead was no Russ Meyer bathing beauty. Her long, dark hair was stringy and cut at a ragged angle, and as the movie flickered before my eyes, I noticed that she was cultivating a wispy Little Richard mustache on her upper lip. Most disconcerting were her eyebrows—or eyebrow—which grew in a straight line across her broad forehead. Whenever she appeared on the screen, Tindall would allude to *The Bride of Frankenstein* by cackling: "More lightning, Igor!"

For an hour and a half, we watched intently as a sleazy, slick-haired con man worked at getting her into bed. In keeping with the best moral traditions of the day, she refused to comply. He took her dancing, the two of them performing a herky-jerky amalgamation of the Monkey, the Swim, and the Funky Broadway at a dance club that made the Castaways look like the Copacabana. In one particularly memorable scene, he spent twenty minutes squirting her with a garden hose while she laughed hysterically, twirling round and round and performing an occasional loop de loop. Then he drove her through the night in his '55 Ford convertible with her damp hair whipping in the wind.

"She'll catch her death riding around like that in the cold night air," Gene observed.

The actress couldn't have spoken more than one or two

complete sentences in the entire film. Mostly she shook her head and mouthed the word "no" to his suggestions that they retire to his apartment for "a good time."

The four of us sat transfixed by the possibility that this woman might have sex with the sleazy antihero, and none of us hit the snack bar for Cokes or popcorn or to use the restroom lest we miss a frame of this cinematic tour de force. We knew she would eventually relent or there'd be a riot at the Starlight Drive-In, and the place would be razed to the ground by angry patrons.

The movie dragged on, the couple strolling along a riverbank hand-in-hand in the moonlight or riding a Honda 90 cc motorcycle down the main street of a dusty little desert town or drinking beer in a biker bar, the interior of which resembled the Tap Room.

"Ok," she said, after an hour-and-a-half of teasing, "I guess it'll be all right."

We leaned forward in unison, our eyes straining in their sockets. The male lead took the actress by the hand, and the two of them ambled into a dilapidated ranch house. He smiled broadly into the wide-angle lens, his eyebrows writhing with Groucho-like approval, and closed the door behind him. The camera zoomed in on a brass pineapple door knocker, and the credits began rolling silently up the screen.

"What the hell!" I heard someone in a nearby car exclaim. The four of us sat there dumbfounded. When the credits ended, a brief silence settled over the rows of cars and pickup trucks tilted into the night sky—and then a single engine roared to life, and for the only time in my considerable drive-in experience, outraged moviegoers flashed their lights and honked their horns in rage and frustration.

"What a gyp!" Tindall said. "I can't believe I wasted a buck and a quarter on that!"

As we rode back to the dorm, Maynard and Gene, who were huddled in the back seat, made up dialogue the couple might have exchanged after they closed the bedroom door—and that's when I realized how much I was going to miss these guys when the semester ended. Nine months earlier we had been strangers to each other, and now we were as close as brothers. I'd had good friends in high school, but I'd lived with these palookas for two semesters. I knew a little of their family histories and they'd shared misfortunes from their high school years, but I thought I understood what they believed and what they didn't. When I heard someone laugh on my end of the hall, I knew who it was. I would miss their quirkiness, their bursts of humor, and mostly, their lies.

As for the cinéma vérité we'd paid good money to experience, it was without a doubt the worst all-time low-rent drive-in movie ever, and that's saying something, but I had to admit, if only to myself, that it was closer to life than the swill Galsworthy was spewing.

• • •

I spent Sunday fiddling with sentences, changing a word here and recopying the entire essay in longhand. I'd worked hard, and I was immensely pleased with myself.

On Monday, May 2, I passed my essay to Betty Gerow, and the following Friday, May 6, she handed it back with a D scrawled in red ink on the top of the first page. A brief note stated that my comparison was "interesting," although I'd failed to prove the connection between Wodehouse and Galsworthy. "Probably Wodehouse is parodying a particular style of English writing popular during the Edwardian period," Gerow wrote, "but there's no evidence that he ever read Galsworthy." In large letters she'd scrawled: "However, you would have earned a B on this essay had there not been so many careless errors!" And she added a zinger: "Do you know that Galsworthy was awarded the Nobel Prize for Literature?"

Mistakes in grammar, spelling, and punctuation had pulled down my grade. I'd been in such a hurry to hand in my essay that I'd failed to proofread carefully. It was embarrassing—two subject-verb disagreements, a sentence fragment, three misspelled words, a pronoun-antecedent error, and three comma splices! I had convinced myself that the greater the length of my essay the better my chances of earning an A or B, but, in fact, the more words I'd written the more errors I'd made. I was lucky not to have gotten an F. How could I have been so foolish? Why didn't I have someone proofread my work? As I studied Gerow's comments, I realized, too, that I'd memorized what I *thought* I'd written, not what was on the page. The more I studied the red marks splattered across my carefully wrought paragraphs, the more convinced I was that my grade was the result of one of my most apparent shortcomings: the tendency to allow my enthusiasm to overwhelm my better judgment. If I didn't get my head together, it was going to be a hard life.

I trudged back to my room. Brinkley was stretched out on his bunk reading, and I collapsed on my bed and stared at the ceiling, allowing the pages of my essay to flutter dramatically to the floor. He let me stew for half an hour before speaking. Then he lifted himself onto one elbow and asked, "What did Gerow give you on your essay?"

"I got a D," I said.

Brinkley laughed. "Told ya."

# Nineteen

When the exam schedule was published, I sat down with a calendar and allotted my study time, concentrating on those courses that demanded extra attention. My last exam, Economic Geography, was scheduled for 8 a.m. on Thursday, May 26, and when I perused the "Need a Ride?" notices thumbtacked to the bulletin board in Mooney, I found, to my disgust, that the jerk who'd given me a lift at Easter was advertising for passengers needing a ride north on the 26th. "Will be leaving at noon," was printed at the bottom of the index card. My last exam would end at 11 a.m. I dreaded suffering another seven-hour trip with the greedy cretin—Lordy, he was charging $12 per person!—but there was no use hanging around until Friday. My friends were anxious to head home for the summer, and there was nothing to keep me on campus a moment longer.

I tried not to dwell on the poor grade I'd received on my Galsworthy essay, concentrating instead on reviewing in detail the stories we'd read and discussed in Gerow's class. Otherwise, I had my loose ends tied up. I'd be seeing Blondie on May 14 for one last outing to the Castaways, and we'd agreed to date during the summer, contingent on my ability to borrow the LeSabre from my father. Most of my coursework was complete. All I had to do was relax, attend classes, take notes, and allow the semester to drift to its inevitable conclusion.

But I was uneasy, vaguely aware that change was in the offing. After nine months, I was in sync with the rhythms of campus life—my classes, Friday night beer at the Tap Room with my friends, meals in McEwen, Saturday nights at the Castaways with Blondie, and most particularly with the cadence of dorm life, which, despite its minor irritations and inconveniences, offered immediate and agreeable companionship. I was perfectly at ease in room 202 on the second floor of Smith Residence Hall, and I wasn't looking forward to relocating and readjusting, even if I was returning to what I had once thought of as home.

I began my transition by sorting through my belongings. Since I'd be riding in a station wagon with three or four other homeward-bound students, I'd have to leave some possessions behind. I decided to abandon three shirts that had seen better days, an old pair of Converse All Stars that I hadn't worn despite Grandmother Drager's good advice, a stack of fall semester textbooks I'd been unable to sell, a broken windup alarm clock, an old gooseneck lamp, and my copy of *The Mouse that Roared*, which I'd never finished reading. A few smaller items I decided to transport home. They were mementos mostly—a pack of Home Run cigarettes, a harmonica in key of C, a Wodehouse novel I was in the process of rereading and other bits and pieces I'd accumulated over the previous nine months. I stashed this detritus in an 8" x 10" cardboard container I'd commandeered from the bookstore, and I carefully tied up my fall semester notebooks with twine and stashed them sidewise in the box, covering everything with my father's Navy blanket, which was unnecessary on warm spring nights.

...

On the afternoon of Monday, May 9—ten days before the end of classes—I was stretched out on my bed reading Hemingway's "The Short Happy Life of Francis Macomber" when Gene stuck his head into the room and said, "Hey, you've got a phone call."

In the nine months I'd been living in the dorm I'd talked twice on the pay phone, which was reserved for long-distance calls, and my first thought was that a relative had died. I stepped into the hall and leaned against the soda machine with the receiver pressed to my ear and said, "Hello."

"What are you doing?" My mother was on the other end of the line.

"Studying."

"I've got some bad news for you. Your friend Barrie Barnes is dead."

Although taken aback, I comprehended instantly what my mother was telling me—Barrie was dead, simple enough—but my first thought was that he'd probably died in an automobile accident. "Dead?" I asked. I needed to respond, if only to repeat what I'd been told. "What do you mean he's dead?"

"I mean he's dead."

"How?"

"He was killed in Vietnam. Norma Lee called this morning and told me what happened."

This news, unexpected as it was, would not have come as a complete surprise if I'd known Barrie was serving in Vietnam. But I didn't. Either my father had neglected to mention Barrie's deployment, or he'd not been told that Barrie was "in country."

We talked for ten minutes, my mother detailing the events leading up to Barrie's death. She explained, employing quasi-military jargon she'd probably picked up from Norma Lee's telling, that his unit was "conducting operations" in a part of Vietnam known as Ho Bo Woods when they "made contact" with the enemy and Barrie was wounded in the leg. He was on a stretcher awaiting evacuation when one of his buddies was hit. Disobeying his sergeant's orders, Barrie grabbed a rifle and ran to rescue his friend and was shot in the chest. He died instantly. End of story.

"I could have predicted this years ago," my mother said. "He never would listen to anyone. Such a bullheaded kid!"

"Is Dad there?" I asked. I wanted to talk to my father. Maybe he could supply a more precise account of what had happened to Barrie—or maybe I simply needed to hear the ring of authority I knew his familiar voice would offer.

"All your father knows is what I told him."

"What can I do?" I asked. I wasn't catching the bus home for the funeral. With exams two weeks away, I couldn't skip a week of classes and expect to pass any of my courses. And what would I say to the Barneses if I phoned them to express condolences? The idea of speaking with a member of Barrie's family terrified me. A Hallmark sympathy card seemed pointless. A schmaltzy line or two, undecipherable, incomprehensible, appearing in their mailbox long after the coffin had been lowered into the earth, was a waste of time and paper. If there was a way to *truly* console Barrie's parents and brother, I would have done so. If I could have brought Barrie back to life, I would have done that too. But beyond these obvious impossibilities, beyond my absolute powerlessness, I needed to make things better for myself.

"There's nothing you or anyone else can do," my mother said. "He's dead and that's all there is to it."

"Please tell the Barneses that I'm very sorry."

An awkward silence followed, and then my mother said, "How

will I ever be able to look Norma Lee in the eye knowing that her son is dead and my son is alive?"

"I don't know," I said. "I need to go. I've got to study for exams."

I closed the door to my room and sat at my desk. I was thankful Brinkley hadn't returned from his weekend in Virginia. I needed to figure things out. Nothing could have been more befuddling than the death of a friend in a war whose purpose I didn't comprehend. Here was a childhood playmate from my idyllic Delmarva days, a middle-American kid, a fellow baby boomer, shot dead at nineteen. I was startled by the obvious possibility that it could have been me cut down in a meaningless skirmish eight thousand miles away from home.

I reviewed the times Barrie and I had spent together, my memory sliding from one image to another in no particular sequence—the hours playing hide-and-seek on dusky evenings in the little town of Easton, Maryland, and summer days I visited with him in Salisbury, where we skipped stones from the banks of the Wicomico. But what I remembered most vividly was a summer afternoon in 1957—we were both eleven—when Barrie and I were singing our favorite top ten rock 'n' roll songs and I mentioned that I was fond of a country song, "The Tennessee Waltz." "I can teach you how to play it on the piano," he said, and then he sat down at the family's upright Baldwin and with uncharacteristic purposefulness showed me how to pick out the melody on the white keys. It was a good moment to hold in memory, affirmative and focused, his casual smile, his fingers walking along the ivories. Beyond that, there wasn't much I could take away from our friendship, little in the way of consolation. My mother, always gifted at breaking life down into its least common denominator, said Barrie was dead and that's all there was to it. She was right.

I'd had another friend, Donnie Harper, who had met an

untimely end, hit by a truck on his tenth birthday as he chased a basketball, a gift from his parents, into the street, life offering up one of its tragic clichés. After receiving the news that Donnie was DOA at the local hospital, my parents and I sat in our living room for an hour and didn't speak. Following that long silence, my young life moved forward. I grew into the empty space his absence left. Now the same was true with Barrie's sudden disappearance. He was gone, taking a little of me with him, but already I felt myself propelled forward.

With Barrie's death, the statistics, the stark cardinal numbers signifying the suffering of the dead and wounded in Vietnam, were made flesh and blood, irrevocably altering my attitude about the war and reinforcing my determination not to willingly participate in it. I had believed, before my mother's phone call, that it was improbable that I'd ever see combat, even if I were drafted. I knew from reading in *Time* and *Newsweek* that there were 300,000 Americans in Vietnam and KIAs were running less than 300 a month, meaning that an incredibly minuscule percent of our troops involved in the war were dying in battle. I'd kept that reassuring math in the back of my mind. Now I realized my reasoning was specious. Moreover, I'd been assuming that the Americans who were doing the fighting and dying were mostly guys seeking adventure. I had friends who were anxious to experience combat. "I want to get over there before it's all over," a high school buddy had told me. And why not? Boys of my generation had grown up crawling around in the weeds with helmet liners and plastic Mattel Tommy guns. TV programs like *Combat!* and Saturday movie matinees featured heroic GIs slaughtering hordes of enemy soldiers.

Why would we worry? If we didn't want to serve, we didn't have to. It was easy to circumvent the draft. College enrollment included a 2-S deferment, and if a kid couldn't afford a four-year college, community colleges were sprouting up around the country. Tuition was cheap, loans were available and admission was open to everyone, even the rural poor and impoverished inner-city kids. Guys who lost their deferments could join the National Guard or the Coast Guard, branches of the service that weren't involved in the fighting in Vietnam. If all else failed, the Canadian border beckoned.

I considered the effect Barrie's death would have upon my father and his insistence that I enlist. A senseless loss so close to home had to give him pause. Surely, he wouldn't want his son to meet a similar fate. On the other hand, he'd taught thousands of midshipmen, and many of them were dying every day in Vietnam. As a matter of principle, he might continue to suggest I join the military.

I didn't mention Barrie's death to my friends on second Smith. It would have served no purpose. I suspected the news that I'd lost a friend in combat might sound as if I were eliciting sympathy or strike my companions as excessively dramatic: "Hey, guess what happened to a good friend of mine?" The spring of '66 was early in the war, and although the weekly casualties were the highest since our involvement in Vietnam, I doubted anyone at Elon could name a friend who'd died in that distant war. I kept the news to myself.

When Tindall asked if I was going to dinner, I said, "Yeah, sure." We joked as usual as we strutted to McEwen Dining Hall and shuffled through the serving line, but as I ate my meatloaf and smiled at the witty small talk, the unhappy news of Barrie's death gnawed at me. On my way back to the dorm, I ducked into the Carlton Building library to leaf through *Time* and *Newsweek*. I wasn't sure what I was looking for. Perhaps I expected to find a timely story relating to the unit action in which my friend had been killed. Maybe there'd be photographs taken during the fighting, and I could garner a sense of how the world appeared to Barrie in his final moments. Whatever I was seeking, I was disappointed. There were brief articles concerning Operation Rolling Thunder, a photo of a Buddhist monk immolating himself, and an op-ed piece on the "Inequities of the Draft," which was hardly news to anyone caught up in the Selective Service System. I stared resentfully at photos of movie stars featured in one of the magazines, tore out two pages and folded them in my shirt pocket. The reading public was more interested in Julie Christie than the combat deaths of American grunts. I found no solace in the written word, so I left the library and strolled back to the dorm in the twilight, marveling at the quiet beauty of a spring evening.

• • •

Which brings me to a gap in my narrative. No period in my young life is clearer in memory than my freshman year in college—except for the last days of class and spring semester exams. My notebooks contain no entries after May 9. Nor do I remember my finals. It's as if I never attended those last few class meetings, although I'm sure I did, and my grades indicate I performed well enough on my exams.

I can't claim that I was grieving for my lost friend, or that I'd become somehow disillusioned. I don't recall being particularly unhappy or introspective or preoccupied. The days simply passed in a blur.

Probably I enjoyed a few beers at the Tap Room with my friends on Friday, May 13, and I'm confident that Blondie and I danced at the Castaways on the evening of May 14. Pressed between blank pages of one of my notebooks is a yellowing napkin on which is scribbled in Blondie's distinctive looping hand: "Give me a call when you get home. We'll go dancing," followed by her phone number in Rockville.

I was tired of studying and sick of taking tests and writing papers. I needed a break, so I began my summer vacation eight days before the semester was over. All I have to offer from that time is an awe-inspiring blank—no tender heart-to-heart conversation with Blondie, no long farewells at the Tap Room, no inspirational advice from my professors. I made no mention of Barrie in the pages of my notebook.

What I do recall is leaving my last exam and hurrying over to second Smith to say goodbye to my friends. Brinkley had long since headed back to Zuni, but I ran into Witt Halle and wished him well. Scott Roberson was in his room busily packing up his belongings, and I shook his hand and thanked him for the umpteenth time for saving my life. I chatted with Gene Matthews and Steve Maynard in their dorm room and promised I'd see them in the fall. But when I went looking for Steve Tindall, I was told he'd driven north earlier that day. I would miss his acerbic wit and keen insights. He'd made me laugh a thousand times.

I collected my gear and toted it down to the parking lot adjacent to Smith, where I found my ride waiting, and paid the driver $12 for the trip north. I had a five-dollar bill and some change in my pocket, the last of my Drug Fair earnings. I tossed my few belongings into the back of the station wagon and climbed into the passenger seat. A couple of other northbound students tumbled into the back, and the overloaded vehicle lumbered to the wrought iron gate through which my parents and I had passed nine months earlier. We paused to allow the traffic to slacken, and as we idled there in the shadow of Smith Residence Hall, I was possessed by the notion that I was stepping out of romance forever, that henceforth the world would be a harsher, less forgiving place.

# Twenty

At precisely 9 a.m. on Friday, May 27, I was banging on a cash register in the express lane at the Eastport Safeway, toting up cans of pickled beets and projecting a cheerful persona. Mr. Short had scheduled me from 9 a.m. to 5 p.m. Monday through Saturday for the entire summer. "You can pick up overtime by restocking baby food and spices on Friday and Saturday evenings. If you're up to it, I'll schedule you for a register from 5 to 9 after your regular hours. Of course, you'll get a supper break," he told me, as if he were doing me a favor.

My fellow workers, most of whom were holdovers from the previous year, regarded me with ironic forbearance. I'd gone off to college, and they assumed I was brimming with new knowledge. They were deferential to a fault and anxious to help me with menial tasks such as sorting returned soda bottles and sweeping the loading dock at the end of a shift. If I had to work—and I did—I was glad to be employed at the Safeway. After all, the place was air-conditioned and was heaven compared to Drug Fair.

I didn't object to the long hours. It was less stressful to be at work than at home enduring the routine annoyances that had only amplified in my absence. After nine months of hassle-free dorm life, I was in no mood to cope with my parents' arbitrary restraints and, most of all, with my sister's rebellious behavior. During my first three weeks at home she stayed out well after her curfew on two occasions, and when our mother expressed concern regarding her behavior, Debbie threatened to run away from home. At least once a week I had to listen to a protracted late-night shouting match. These arguments blew in and out like the thunderstorms that swept off the Chesapeake, violent and unexpected, and after my sister had slammed her bedroom door with all her might and the rafters had ceased rattling I'd hear my mother and father, their room next to the one Mike and I shared, communicating in mumbles—my father's voice deep but steady, my mother's an aggrieved twitter in the darkness. Mike and I steered clear of these mêlées, but I found these disagreements pointless and vaguely unsettling, even if they didn't involve me.

My father, much to my surprise, had grown forbearant, finding little fault with my sullen behavior and lauding my spring semester grades when they arrived in the mail. "Not nearly as bad as I expected," he said, offering what was for him effusive praise. He even went so far as to give me a gentle pat on the back. "How's it going?" he asked one evening after I stumbled in from a 12-hour shift. Perhaps he suspected that the death of my friend had darkened my mood, and he wanted to avoid making my life any gloomier, but I felt only a suspicious resentment.

My brother was, as always, cheerful. We shared the upstairs front bedroom, and in the evenings he'd tune in WCAO on a leather-cased AMC portable transistor radio he'd appropriated from our sister, who no longer had time for such foolishness. I half-listened to rock 'n' roll while reading in my latest Wodehouse book. I'd focus briefly on a page or two and drift off to the ominous strains of Barry Sadler's "Ballad of the Green Berets" or the sulky jive of Question Mark and The Mysterians' "96 Tears."

My mother, always a penny-pinching child of the Depression, insisted I pay her $35 a month to live at home, an amount I considered excessive. "You're an adult now," she said. "Pay your own way." I didn't protest, even when she announced that I'd be expected to save enough money to pay my tuition, room, board and books for the fall semester. I made a few calculations and concluded that achieving such a goal was impossible, even if I worked every second the Safeway was open and saved every penny I earned. I'd probably have to land another job when I returned to Elon in the fall. But what could I do but shrug and bide my time? So each morning I ironed a white shirt and khaki slacks, clipped on my black bow tie, pinned my plastic name tag to my shirt pocket and trudged up Bay Ridge Avenue in the ever-intensifying heat and humidity to the Eastport shopping center, where I'd stand behind my cash register checking out groceries ad infinitum, ad nauseam.

The days passed with such soul-numbing regularity that I grew to appreciate the occasional evil-eyed vigilante who claimed I'd overcharged him or her. "What did you ring up for that can of sauerkraut?" a churlish customer would ask. I'd smile, maintaining a noble impassivity as I summoned Mr. Short over the PA—"Manager to checkout seven"—so he could verify the register tape. "See," he'd say, a satisfied grin on his smug, bony face, "here's the amount you were charged—exactly what's indicated on the can." I was glad for these distractions, which served to transport me from the moment. I missed my buds on second Smith, beer at the Tap Room, and the freedom college afforded, a life that was, when compared to my present situation, all air and ease. I especially missed Blondie, and I thought about her constantly as I bagged tons of groceries. I wondered if she'd found a summer job. Mostly I worried that she might be seeing someone else. My mother didn't allow long-distance calls—"The phone bill is sky high," she claimed—so I suppressed the urge to dial Blondie's number in Rockville. I didn't know anyone who'd loan me a car and there was no chance I could borrow the LeSabre, so a visit to Rockville was an impossibility. But I remained mildly philosophical, viewing my circumstance as an unpleasant interlude I'd have to endure on my way to better times.

• • •

On the fourth Wednesday in June, I stumbled into the house at 9:30 p.m., dead beat after an overtime shift, and found the old man stretched out on the couch in his white boxer shorts and T-shirt, a sphygmomanometer wrapped around his bicep and a stethoscope dangling from his neck. As the pneumatic screened door shushed shut behind me, he sat on the edge of the couch and carefully placed the medical paraphernalia on the antique lard bench my parents had repurposed as a coffee table.

"I want to talk to you," he said.

"What's wrong?" I asked.

"What makes you think something's wrong?"

I didn't respond but sat down in the wingback chair next to the door and waited for what I thought would be a reprimand for an unintended infraction.

"How long did you work today?" he asked.

"Twelve hours."

"You've been working six days a week?"

"Yeah, I have."

He shook his head and groaned. "Saving any money?"

"Every cent, except for what I have to pay Mom."

"That's a lot of hours."

"Yeah, it is."

"I've noticed how hard you've been working. And I have to admit you had a pretty good year at college."

"Thanks." I was waiting for the other shoe to drop.

"Well, I've decided you can use the car one night each weekend, if your mother and I don't have plans."

I could hardly credit what I was hearing. "I can borrow the LeSabre?"

"There are a couple of conditions."

"What?"

"The car has to be in the driveway by 12:30 and not a second later, and I do not want you to put the top down."

"Is that it?"

"That's it."

"Can I use the car this Friday night?"

"I don't see why not."

"Thanks," I said.

I immediately started up the stairs to my room. It was wise to disappear before he changed his mind.

"Hey," my father called after me. "Do you ever think about your friend Barrie?"

I turned on the steps and looked back at my father, stretched out again on the couch, his face bathed in the amber illumination from the table lamp. "Yeah, I do," I said.

"I'll tell you what: if you need some extra money for tuition in the fall, I'll see that you get it."

"Thanks," I said. "I could use the help."

"It's a shame," he said, "about your friend."

If my father expressed affection or sorrow, it was always in shades of reserve. How imperfectly I understood him.

• • •

The following day during my lunch break, I dialed Blondie's Rockville number using the pay phone outside Mr. Short's office. I deposited a stack of coins in the designated slots and when a woman answered, I asked for Blondie.

"She's not available," the woman responded politely. "May I tell her who called?"

I told the disembodied voice who I was, wondering if Blondie had ever mentioned me to her family.

"Oh," she said, "you're her friend from college. She's anxious to talk with you. She's been waiting tables at breakfast and lunch at a dinette. Why don't you call back after five?"

The phone call, however brief, put a spring in my step. The woman I'd spoken with had acknowledged that Blondie was "anxious" to talk with me. I'd been on her mind, and I was buoyed by this revelation. But the afternoon seemed to drag on interminably until Mr. Short released me for a dinner break, and I carefully dialed the Rockville number again. Blondie answered.

"How are you?" I asked.

"Fine," she said. "Why haven't you called?" There was an echo on the line—what my mother called a "satellite connection"—and Blondie sounded remote, as if she were speaking at the far end of a dark tunnel.

I explained that I'd been putting in twelve-hour days at work and mentioned my mother's dictate concerning long-distance calls. "I don't have any news. I've been stuck here at the Safeway," I said. "Would you like to go dancing this Friday night?"

She was silent, and then replied with what I perceived as a notable lack of enthusiasm, "Friday night would be fine."

"We can go to the Bayou in Georgetown," I said. "It's the best rock 'n' roll club on the planet. You'll love it."

Blondie gave me directions to an apartment complex on Mt.

Vernon Place in Rockville, and I promised to be at her door no later than 7:30 p.m., if traffic on Interstate 95 didn't interfere.

"I'll be ready," she said and hung up.

I begged off overtime on Friday evening—"I could use a night off," was sufficient explanation for Mr. Short to send me on my way—and after closing out my register at 5 p.m., I double-timed it home to shower and dress in my best khakis and a perfectly faded madras shirt. At 6:30 p.m. I was blasting up John Hanson Highway, the LaSabre's speedometer edging ten miles an hour over the speed limit. It took me an hour to make the Rockville exit and another fifteen minutes to locate Blondie's apartment in a generic block of rectangular brick buildings of the type that were beginning to clog the DC suburbs.

I rang the doorbell twice in quick succession, impatient for our evening to begin, but when Blondie opened the door and stepped out into the late afternoon sun, I was momentarily nonplussed. Her long blond hair, the entangled sheaves of curls that had first attracted me, was cropped close on the back and sides and shorn to an inch or two on top into what might be kindly described as a "Twiggy." I could hear her friends saying, "I love what you've done with your hair; it's sooooo cute!" But I was not charmed; in fact, I found this unexpected metamorphosis alarming. Where once there'd been an instantaneous connection between us, there was now a disconcerting emotional vacancy, and it occurred to me that her enveloping locks had been a third presence in our relationship, a tangled, enticing entity that had danced with us on nights at the Castaways. I keenly felt its absence. Her neck appeared longer and thinner than I recalled, and her head, noticeably tilted as if marveling at an object on the far horizon, seemed larger, her blue eyes fuller, deeper. Still, she shone through the incongruity, her unframed face graced with a familiar quizzical smile and touched with an almost invisible application of makeup. She was dressed in a low-cut, sky-blue summer blouse, beige wraparound skirt and strapless, toe-thong sandals—beautiful as ever, despite the alarming transformation.

"It's good to see you," she said and hugged me gently, a smile lingering on her lips as she slipped imperceptibly from my arms. She hurried me away from her front door and to the car with a nervous, impetuous gesture, sparing me an awkward first meeting with her parents and siblings. As we pulled onto the highway, she asked, "Do you like my haircut?"

I didn't, but said I did. I wasn't going to offer any opinion that might jeopardize our first evening together in a month.

"All that hair in this hot weather!" she exclaimed. "It was too uncomfortable. And I had to wear a hairnet while waitressing. I'm too vain for that." She rambled on awkwardly about the tribulations of diner work. "There's a lunch bar and ten booths and not much in the way of tips, but it's the only job I could find that's in walking distance of the apartment...."

"How do you like the car?" I asked, fishing for a compliment as if the LeSabre was my personal property.

"Oh, yeah," she said, with a cursory look around. "Nice."

It was a straight thirty-minute shot down Washington National Pike to Georgetown and the Bayou. As we traveled south, I noticed that our usually effortless conversation had become stilted. I asked about her family and friends, and she skillfully steered me away from the personal, grousing about the minor irritations of life at home. Perhaps it was the four weeks we'd been apart or the new surroundings in which we found ourselves, but there was a palpable change in her demeanor. A vague, static energy had imposed itself between us.

The Bayou was a nightspot I'd frequented with a fake ID

during my junior and senior years in high school. The club occupied a two-story brick building on K Street under the Whitehurst Freeway. Railroad tracks sliced down the Potomac side of the brick street, and the elevated roadway cast the cavernous space below in a sinister murkiness that echoed with the rumble of the traffic above. The neon-illumined entrance to the club required an upward step or two before passing through double doors into a large vestibule occupied by a cashier and a brawny bouncer. Rock 'n' roll pounded from the dance floor beyond, beckoning us inward. I paid the outrageous six-dollar cover charge, and we squirmed into the high-ceilinged, dimly lighted room crowded with writhing bodies. The upwardly evolving space seemed to extend into infinity, and a wide stage fronted the room.

The Telstars, a four-piece band of miscreants with colossal swept-back pompadours and thin pockmarked faces, rocked the room from floor to rafter. The ground level was furnished with thirty or forty tables occupied by patrons who were there to party. Blondie and I were ushered up a broad flight of worn wooden stairs built into an ancient stone wall to the second floor, where we were seated at a rickety table flush against a rail barrier that afforded an aerial view of the dancers below. The clientele appeared to be mostly Georgetown bohemians, a mix of eccentrics and college students like us, everyone writhing in free-form celebration.

The Bayou projected an otherworldly ambiance that contrasted starkly with the mundane low-ceilinged Castaways, lost for now in the Carolina boondocks. The Telstars were a thunderous boom-boom rock 'n' roll band, rattling the mercury fillings in my molars. The interior structure of the club, the flat-black brick walls and invisible ceiling, ricocheted every excruciating note blasting from a giant bank of amps. Covers of top-ten hits—"We Can Work It Out," "Good Lovin'," "Hanky Panky," "Paint It Black,"

"Wild Thing"—were identifiable only by the bass lines reverberating in my bones. The Bayou was no soul-music club populated by prissy dancers demonstrating their slickest shuffle; the Georgetown crowd was a spontaneous assemblage of loose-jointed spirits pulsating amoeba-like on the dance floor below us.

"This place is the coolest," Blondie shouted across the table.

After consuming a couple of longnecks, we cautiously descended the dark stairs to the dance floor, where Blondie melted like a chameleon into the crowd. Among this mass of revelers there was no dress code, no standard dance step, no one to emulate, no rules whatsoever—and Blondie was instantly a part of the Bayou's frantic commotion. I'd never seen her happier. She was lost in the jam of bodies, fluttering away like a freed bird. Her wild animation, which was starkly out of place at the Castaways, attracted no attention at the Bayou. She was part of a heterogeneous whole, instantly accepted. I worked to keep up with her as she whirled into the crowd swaying to "Do You Believe in Magic," and "What Goes On," but she took little notice of my efforts, caught up as she was in the motion of swaying bodies.

We danced for over an hour. When the Telstars took a break, we straggled back to our table and ordered another round. Blondie smiled and motioned to the crowd milling on the dance floor. "They're so kind to each other," she said.

"Kind?" I asked. "What do you mean?"

"The way they dance. There's no right or wrong way to it."

That's when I understood what she meant when she'd said months earlier that the Shag was "not fair." For every kid who danced at the Castaways, there were thousands like Sarah Jean in her wrinkled blue dress and white go-go boots, who couldn't. They didn't have the skill or the money or anyone to invite them onto the dance floor. The Shag was exclusionary. Blondie's dance steps, whatever they were, required no expertise, only a sense of rhythm and the confidence to be oneself. At the Bayou there was no hurtful distinction between those who were great dancers and those who weren't.

When the Telstars cranked up again, we took to the floor and danced away another 45 minutes. I gave my watch an occasional cautionary glance, and, at 11 p.m., I suggested we head back to Rockville. "I hate to leave, but I'd like to be home by 12:30," I explained.

We shared a last dance to a cover of the Outsiders' "Time Won't Let Me," and then slipped out into the sudden rush of city heat, the music dying away as we hurried to the LeSabre. We pulled out onto the Capital Beltway and then hit I-270 north, the radio blaring.

"Would you like to do this again next Friday or Saturday night?" I asked. I was certain Blondie would say yes. But she didn't respond immediately, turning to stare out the passenger-side window at the passing city. I couldn't help but observe a nuance of gesture, a cheerless forbearance that brought me to a realization that we were at the end of something.

"I can't go dancing with you anymore," she said, her voice clear and definite.

I turned off the radio. "What do you mean?"

"I mean I can't see you again."

I fell silent, searching for words, any words, that might extricate me from this startling predicament. *I can't see you again.* What had I done to elicit an unqualified exclusion from her life? We had never argued or exchanged an unpleasant word, never suffered a disagreeable moment together. But I knew already how this conversation would end: I'd be the aggrieved party in what was becoming, at that moment, another melancholy love story.

"Why? Why can't we see each other again?"

"The truth is," she said, "I've been seeing an old high school friend—he's in grad school at GW—and I told him that I needed to tell you this in person, not over the phone, that I owed you an honest explanation."

"You've been going out with him this summer?"

"Yes."

"And we can't go dancing again, ever?"

"It's just not fair to you—or to him—for us to keep seeing each other."

Cars zoomed by us on the Interstate, semis flashed their high beams in my rearview, and I felt wholly abandoned, desperate. Then it occurred to me that this news might only be a temporary setback. "Maybe we can start going to the Castaways again when we get back to college." The faint spark of hope in my voice surprised even me.

"I'm not going back," she said, immediately, "at least not to North Carolina. I'm transferring to the University of Maryland in January."

"You won't be at school in the fall?" I was incredulous.

"No. I'm working in the fall to save money."

As we drew nearer our destination, I pled my case with all the logic I could muster, but Blondie calmly and directly rebuffed my every suggestion and concession, and each passing mile drove me deeper into defeat. By the time we pulled up in front of her apartment building, I'd exhausted every possible point of negotiation. I parked the LeSabre and cut the engine. "If things don't work out with your friend, give me call," I suggested in a final attempt to mend what Blondie had irreparably shattered.

"It's best to end this before it becomes too painful."

"It's already painful," I admitted.

"I want you to smile when you remember me," she said, placing her hand lightly on my shoulder. "I know I'll always have fond memories of the time we've spent together."

"You're sure about this?"

"I am."

I'd hoped to detect a trace of doubt in her final answer, but there was none. I understood even then that women are wiser about affairs of the heart, and what dignity I possessed weighed against my stupefaction. I didn't attempt to persuade her further. I walked her to the front stoop, and we hugged for the last time. She stepped inside and closed the door. I walked back to the LeSabre, dropped the convertible top and blasted back to Annapolis at speeds that should have landed me in the slammer—or the morgue. Careering east on John Hanson Highway, the Mamas and the Papas' "I Saw Her Again" came on the radio and the song's tenuous narrative seemed to fit my circumstance, except the first line that should have gone "I saw *him* again last night. . . ." As I pulled onto Bay Ridge Avenue, three blocks from home, "Summer in the City" came pounding over WCAO and I maxed out the volume.

• • •

I moped around for a few days, feeling sorry for myself. But I didn't grieve overly much. I was young, resilient, and Blondie's reasoned explanation for our parting had been forthright and gentle. I found it impossible to harbor a trace of bitterness. I worked out the summer at the Safeway, dating local girls, secretly stashing away a chunk of overtime money to buy a used car. When I headed south in September, it was with the knowledge that I'd never live in Annapolis again.

Back on campus, I was assigned a freshly painted room in Hook Residence Hall, but it took only a day or two to realize that many of my freshman friends were absent. Steve Tindall had transferred to the University of Delaware. Witt Halle and Scott Roberson had disappeared without explanation. Only Gene Matthews and Steve Maynard remained, survivors of the ancient regime, my only buddies from the old second Smith crew. I'd make new friends during the next three years, but none were quite as authentic as my freshman cronies.

I often thought of Blondie, especially when I had occasion to visit West dorm, where I could picture her stepping into the dimly lighted lounge, her face aglow with a sudden smile and an endearing touch of self-assurance. I'd date other women, a few seriously, but Blondie remains a singular presence in my memory of that time.

I never mastered the finer points of dancing the Shag, and I didn't set foot inside the Castaways again. But on a cold January afternoon during my junior year, Gene Matthews and I drove to Greensboro in his dilapidated Ford Falcon to have a couple of Sunday afternoon brews at Ham's drive-in. We drove west on Rt. 70, the path Blondie and I had traveled in the cranky little Renault Dauphine. The trees were bare and the roadside houses and churches seemed unfamiliar. As we approached Bessemer Avenue, I asked Gene to turn right onto Arnold.

"Go slow," I said, as we rolled down the empty street.

"What are we looking for?" Gene asked.

"There it is," I said, pointing to the gray brick building with the Castaways sign propped awkwardly on the sky-flattened roof.

"Oh, yeah," he said, "that's the club where you and that blond girl used to go dancing."

"That's it."

"In the daylight, it looks like any other low-rent dive," he observed.

Gene was right; it was grim—the dull Perma-Stone façade, the gravel parking lot strewn with crumpled beer cans, discarded fast-food wrappers and crushed dreams—all the bleaker in the dusty January sunshine.

"The place hasn't changed at all," I said.

Closing my eyes I could see Blondie and me stepping expectantly through the unfamiliar doorway, her arm locked in mine, and I visualized the interior of the club as I'd first seen it—the tilted tables, the worn wooden dance floor, the couples clutching foolishly at one another, the feverish, restless essence of our time together: all that life and energy gone forever.

"She was a crazy one, wasn't she?" Gene asked.

"She was a dancer," I said.

As we turned the corner, I looked over my shoulder and caught a final flickering glimpse of the old club as it faded from my life, and it came to me that nothing about the Castaways was as splendid as the entrance.

# About the Author

Stephen E. Smith was born in Easton, Maryland, in 1946. After graduating from Elon College, he attended the University of North Carolina at Greensboro, where he received his MFA in 1971. His poems, stories, columns, and reviews have appeared in many periodicals and anthologies. He is the author of nine books of poetry and prose and is the recipient of the Poetry Northwest Young Poet's Prize, the Zoe Kincaid Brockman Prize for poetry, and four North Carolina Press awards. He is also a three-time winner of the Kerrville Folk Festival New Folk Competition for songwriting. He lives in Southern Pines, North Carolina and contributes columns, reviews, and features to *PineStraw, Walter,* and *O.Henry* magazines and occasionally plays guitar and sings the old songs with friends at the Weymouth Center for the Arts and Humanities.

Apprentice House is the country's only campus-based, student-staffed book publishing company. Directed by professors and industry professionals, it is a nonprofit activity of the Communication Department at Loyola University Maryland.

Using state-of-the-art technology and an experiential learning model of education, Apprentice House publishes books in untraditional ways. This dual responsibility as publishers and educators creates an unprecedented collaborative environment among faculty and students, while teaching tomorrow's editors, designers, and marketers.

Eclectic and provocative, Apprentice House titles intend to entertain as well as spark dialogue on a variety of topics. Financial contributions to sustain the press's work are welcomed. Contributions are tax deductible to the fullest extent allowed by the IRS.

To learn more about Apprentice House books or to obtain submission guidelines, please visit www.apprenticehouse.com.

Apprentice House Press
Communication Department
Loyola University Maryland
4501 N. Charles Street
Baltimore, MD 21210
Ph: 410-617-5265
info@apprenticehouse.com • www.apprenticehouse.com

www.ingramcontent.com/pod-product-compliance
Lightning Source LLC
Chambersburg PA
CBHW070609170426
43200CB00012B/2632